# ASIAN BUSINESS WISDOM

# WISDOM

## *From Deals to Dot.Coms*

### *Revised Edition*

# ASIAN BUSINESS WISDOM

## From Deals to Dot.Coms

A collection of timeless success stories
from leading CEOs

Edited by

*Dinna Louise C. Dayao*

**Revised Edition**

**John Wiley & Sons (Asia) Pte Ltd**

Singapore   New York   Chichester
Brisbane   Toronto   Weinheim

This publication is designed to provide accurate and authoritative information in regard to the subject matter covered. It is sold with the understanding that the Publisher is not engaged in rendering professional services. If professional advice or other expert assistance is required, the services of a competent professional person should be sought.

*Other Wiley Editorial Offices*

John Wiley & Sons, Inc., 605 Third Avenue, New York, NY 10158-0012, USA
John Wiley & Sons Ltd, Baffins Lane, Chichester, West Sussex PO19 1UD, England
John Wiley & Sons (Canada) Ltd, 22 Worcester Road, Rexdale, Ontario M9W 1L1, Canada
John Wiley & Sons Australia Ltd, 33 Park Road (PO Box 1226), Milton, Queensland 4046, Australia
Wiley-VCH, Pappelallee 3, 69469 Weinheim, Germany

*Library of Congress Cataloging-in-Publication Data:*


0-471-47911-X (Paper)

Typeset in 11/15 point, Goudy by Linographic Services Pte Ltd
Printed in Singapore by Craft Print Pte Ltd
10 9 8 7 6 5 4 3 2 1

For my parents,
Gregorio Jr. and Concepcion C. Dayao

# Contents

# Acknowledgments

Most of this book was edited in glorious solitude, in an airy room with a window offering a view of the Makati (Philippines) skyline, which, on clear days, still takes my breath away. That doesn't mean that I did everything by myself. My heartfelt thanks and appreciation go to the following:

**John Wiley & Sons:** Nick Wallwork and Janis Soo, for their encouragement and guidance. Tess Bacalla, for being an enthusiastic and critical copyeditor. John Wiley author Leo Gough, for taking the time to share his editing know-how with me even if we are only e-mail acquaintances. Peter Krass, whose best-selling John Wiley-published works, *The Book of Business Wisdom* and *The Book of Leadership Wisdom*, served as invaluable benchmarks.

**Moral supporters:** Sylvia Garde, Rowena Lopez, Sofie Mantuano, Nelia Paculan, and Enid Reyes for sharing their insights, expertise, and friendship.

**Sources:** The visionary CEOs who had the foresight to express their ideas on paper and took the time to participate in this book project.

**Special:** The members of the wonderful family I was blessed to be born into, for their continued love and support. The One Intelligence in the Universe, who gave me everything that I needed in the "right time, space, and sequence" to turn this book into a reality.

# Preface

How would you like the chance to sit down with some of Asia's best and brightest CEOs and hear their hard-earned, practical, and timeless insights into fundamental business processes and their formula for success? Just imagine having the unique opportunity to learn not only from today's movers and shakers, but from yesterday's legends as well.

But, some of you may wonder, what lessons can chief executives from a region that has just bounced back from a financial crisis impart? A lot of valuable instructions, specifically in managing in tough times. CEOs such as Singapore Airlines' Cheong Choong Kong, The Minor Group's William Heinecke, and Giordano's Peter Lau share management principles that can benefit not only ailing companies but even healthy ones. Taking advantage of the crisis to build new alliances and streamline their businesses, they applied strategies that have enabled their companies not only to survive the economic turmoil but to emerge more competitive and with healthy bottom lines.

*Asian Business Wisdom* offers you the rare opportunity to benefit from the diverse experiences of 31 influential Asian CEOs who have successfully grown, managed, and, in some cases, revived their companies.

As you read the book, you will soon find out that the term "Asian" is used quite liberally in this book. It refers to:

- top managers of homegrown companies, such as Acer Group's Stan Shih and Ayala Corporation's Jaime Augusto Zobel de Ayala II;
- CEOs of Asian heritage who head companies outside of their home countries, such as McKinsey's Rajat Gupta and Kleiner Perkins Caufield & Byers' Vinod Khosla; and
- head honchos of Asian subsidiaries of multinational companies, such as McCann-Erickson Philippines' Emily Abrera, Nobuyuki Idei (Sony Corp), and Unilever Thai Holdings' Ralph Kugler.

*Asian Business Wisdom* is divided into five sections. In "Success Principles," featured CEOs share the bedrock beliefs that help them successfully run not just their businesses but also their personal lives. In "Instilling Corporate Culture," they address the processes involved in turning abstract values into an environment that fosters initiative while encouraging people to work toward common goals.

In the section on "The Entrepreneurial Spirit," seasoned company founders delve into the challenges of starting one's own business and staying nimble despite a company's growing size and scope. Here you will also learn about Grameen Bank's Muhammad Yunus's insights into "social entrepreneurship."

In "Tough Business Challenges," dynamic CEOs detail how they have successfully coped with the formidable tasks involved in turnaround management, doing business in China and the new economy, globalization, and knowledge management.

Finally, in "Marketing and Customer Service Strategies," topnotch CEOs debunk advertising and marketing myths and provide case studies of effective techniques. They also share insights into how some customer service exemplars fulfill their customers' needs and make quality service a way of life.

Each article is accompanied by a brief introduction that highlights its author's life and business achievements. Wherever possible, it also includes a list of online resources to direct you to the featured company's Web site, articles on the Internet which complement or provide a counterpoint to the article, and related publications and organizations.

To be sure this book will give you an inside look into the key decision points, breakthrough insights, and proven strategies of some of the region's leading CEOs. Having said this, the author would much appreciate your taking the time to drop her a line and send her your comments and suggestions.

There would be no sweeter reward for her than to learn that her book has delivered on its promise. May reading this book challenge and inspire you as you travel on your own road to business success!

*Dinna Louise C. Dayao*
*dinnadayao@hotmail.com*

# PART 1
# MANAGEMENT PHILOSOPHIES

# A Passion for Success

## Kazuo Inamori

*Founder and Chairman Emeritus, Kyocera Corporation*
*Founder, DDI Corporation*
*Japan*

"Sincerity begets trust, trust begets respect, and respect enables you to lead your group."

**Kazuo Inamori**

Kazuo Inamori, 69, founded high-technology Kyocera Corporation using US$10,000 from a friend whose sole stipulation was "never be a slave to money." Launched in 1959 with only 28 employees, the company has grown into a leading manufacturer of semiconductor parts and telecommunications and electronics products with 14,000 employees and a net income of US$489 million in 2000. Kyocera also owns 25% of DDI Corporation, Japan's number two telecommunications company.

Inamori, listed by London's *Financial Times* as one of the world's 20 most respected business leaders in 1998, believes strongly in "doing what is right" in his entrepreneurial business activities. His civic-mindedness is reflected in Kyocera's corporate motto: *Kei-Ten Ai-Jin*, or "respect the divine and love people." He sprinkles his conversation with proverbs about the importance of consideration for others and thinking about the good of society. "These sayings have formed the philosophical foundation of a tremendous business drive and self-confidence that have been the source of Inamori's success," reports *Financial Times*.

Inamori's pious streak led him to become a Zen monk in 1997. "The precepts of Buddhism are something that management can learn and gain a lot from," he says in an interview. Though he had previously announced his intentions to devote the remainder of his life to "cultivating his soul quietly," Inamori says he will continue to offer advice and guidance to Kyocera and DDI, based on his own mixture of business skills and philosophy.

In his book *A Passion for Success* (McGraw-Hill, 1995) from which the following excerpt is taken, Inamori shares the philosophies by which he has lived and worked for four decades—philosophies that can transform the very nature of business for enterprises and individuals alike.

### Are Leaders Born or Trained?

I have often pondered this question. I think the answer is "both." Just as there are natural athletes, musicians, or artists, there are people born with a natural ability for leadership and charisma. However, I also believe that almost all people can train themselves to be good, if not outstanding, leaders. What is more important than ability is the effort leaders make and the fundamental truths and principles upon which their leadership is based. The most tragic case is a competent leader with a negative way of thinking who leads his or her group astray or into self-destruction.

### My Success Mindset

I do not give up until I am satisfied with a project. Failure is a state of mind. I don't start a major project unless I am thoroughly convinced that it is truly worthwhile. Then I don't have reason to give it up when I encounter an obstacle. If one way is not successful, I search for another until I find a way to get to the true goal behind the project. Sometimes I have to be patient.

### How to Manage Unproductive Workers

We all have differences in ability. Some workers are extremely capable and other workers are less so. As long as workers remain positive and make sincere efforts, managers should treat them well, regardless of their ability to contribute. Managers need to identify workers' strengths and find a place in the organization where they can contribute more.

When we find workers who have a negative attitude, we try to talk to them. We try to show how essential a positive attitude is for us as individuals as well as for the company. In an extreme case, we may even suggest that they find another company or occupation where they can feel more positive and, thus, productive. Those workers who continue to have a negative attitude tend to leave the company naturally after a while.

## Daily Efforts and Yearly Plans

Throughout my life, I have always believed that the best way to predict the future is to work earnestly every day and to look at tomorrow as the extension of our daily efforts. In other words, if you want tomorrow to turn out as you hope it will, you must work hard today and accomplish what you set out to do. At Kyocera, we mostly rely upon our yearly master plans. I believe it is important to have a vision of where we are heading. But a long-term plan will make us into liars as often as it may make us look like prophets.

## Sincerity as a Leadership Quality

Sincerity begets trust, trust begets respect, and respect enables you to lead your group. We often think of respect as something bestowed upon teachers or professors. It is rather unusual to think of respect as being essential to business executives. However, to bring your subordinates together, draw the very best from them, and develop their abilities, you must share a working relationship based on mutual trust. This mutual trust cannot occur unless the leader is a considerate person who is sincere and cares about others.

## Earning the Respect—More than the Trust—of Customers

Obviously, respect and trust go hand in hand—but there is a difference. Trust is a basic prerequisite of doing business. Respect, on the other hand, is an elevated status that is much more difficult to earn.

When customers respect you, they are willing to listen to your opinions and suggestions. Instead of just giving you orders for their current needs, your customers will start to consult you about how best to design their new products. For example, if you are a components supplier, a customer who truly respects you may consult with you in the early design phases of his newest products.

Your future business will be "designed in" because they respect your professional ability, commitment, and, above all, your personal integrity.

## Creating a Clear Vision

I personally try to concentrate on a goal so intently that it becomes programmed into my subconscious mind, which can model and simulate ideas. Anyone with a sufficiently strong desire can do the same. What is important is to continue working on our dream regardless of what we now lack. When we started Kyocera, we spent months planning, dreaming, reflecting, and arguing. When we started DDI Corporation (Japan's first private telecommunications company founded in 1984), we did the same. Today, DDI is considered as the most successful challenger to the former monopoly held by Nippon Telegraph and Telephone.

We started DDI with five extremely competent young engineers from NTT. Every weekend, these five engineers would travel from Tokyo to Kyoto. We spent the weekends at Kyocera's guest house, discussing how to build DDI and make it a success. We continued this every weekend for six months, until our vision started to become clear.

Only after our vision had become so clear that we were convinced of its viability did I decide to go ahead. We faced many obstacles, but our clear vision always found a way around them. We had no real anxiety. Rather, we had confidence that our dream would come true. Ten years later, in 1994, DDI reached consolidated annual sales of almost US$3.8 billion, with a pre-tax profit of US$507 million.

## Drawing Courage from Convictions

I find strength in holding deep personal convictions. I believe others do as well. Incredible strength is often required to do the right thing. If there is even a hint of a misgiving or reluctance, confidence is shaken and courage is lost.

I was once told that 99% of all physicians refuse to diagnose and treat their own loved ones in the event of a serious illness, especially one requiring surgery. Many reasons have been cited to explain this. Perhaps surgeons fear that their hands may hesitate or that their own emotions may make them too unsteady to perform a delicate operation on a loved one.

Their feelings get in their way, and they would rather trust the skill of a colleague than their own.

But that should not be so. If you have true courage and confidence in your skill as a physician, you may not turn your loved ones to your colleagues but perform the very best operation yourself.

One key to finding strength is to have the courage to remain completely objective. Another is to believe in your ability with a conviction that goes deeper than your own emotions.

## Promoting Innovation

First, I ask everybody to make today better than yesterday, then make tomorrow better than today. This is what we call *kaizen*. Second, as the head of the enterprise, I must lead the way by personally being creative and encouraging others to follow. Third, I pay special attention to making sure such efforts continue every day, incessantly, 365 days a year. Finally, I avoid looking for a magical "quick fix" that will make the company grow. Instead, I try to rely on daily innovative efforts to develop the enterprise naturally.

## Innovation in Start-up Firms

This is when innovation becomes absolutely critical. Kyoto Ceramic, Ltd., as Kyocera was originally named, was founded in 1959. Its core was what is now called our Fine Ceramics Group.

From the beginning, this group had always adopted unique ideas. We explored new applications in semiconductors, fishing rods, ceramic knives, and virtually any promising area. The most successful of our applications was the ceramic package for integrated circuits. At that time, making high-quality ceramic packages by sandwiching electrodes between thin ceramic sheets, and then laminating and sintering them, was a completely novel idea. Experts told us we could not do it. By 1994, however, our yearly sales of semiconductor packages had reached US$1 billion.

Later, I came up with the idea of developing a ceramic heater expanding on the same laminating technology employed for semiconductor packages. Today, Kyocera's ceramic heaters are accepted worldwide as original and unique products in automobiles and other applications, having a total worth of over US$50 million.

## Optimism During Hard Times

A leader must always be cheerful and positive—especially in the gloom of a recession. The way to do this is to remain convinced of the viability of your own vision and to share this conviction with your subordinates. In difficult times, it is especially important to see reality as it is and to devise strategies that are best suited to the situation at hand. Remember that the economy runs in cycles and, therefore, an optimistic leader—someone who expects a recession to turn around—can lead the group toward a more positive direction than a pessimist who expects things to grow continually worse. ■

---

The biographical sketch was drawn using the following sources:

Nakamoto, Michiyo. "Single-Minded Devotion." *Financial Times:* November 30, 1998.
Takayama, Hideko. "A Zen Monk on the Board." *Newsweek:* March 1, 1999.

# Online Resources

- **Featured company**
Kyocera Corporation
http://www.kyocera.co.jp/index-e.html

- **Related article**
"Study Entrepreneurial Leadership!"
By Thad Wawro
Many pundits have offered opinions on what makes an entrepreneur successful. The author presents his insights on the main tenets of entrepreneurial leadership philosophy.
http://www.mgeneral.com/3-now/00-now/080008tw.htm

- **Related Web site**
Asian Innovation Awards
By the editors of *Far Eastern Economic Review*
The Asian Innovation Awards honor individuals and companies in Asia who come up with new ideas, methods, or technologies, or apply existing knowledge in a way that improves quality of life and enhances productivity.
http://203.105.48.72/aia/aia.html

# Managing by Detached Involvement

## Jagdish Parikh

*Founder, Centre for Executive Renewal*
*Managing Director, Lemuir Group of Companies*
*India*

"You can never manage effectively that to which you are attached. Any object of addiction will dominate you."

**Jagdish Parikh**

Jagdish Parikh is a leading authority on the interface between life and work. For more than 21 years, Parikh, founder of the Centre for Executive Renewal and co-founder of the World Business Academy, has been enlightening individuals and organizations around the world on topics such as intuition and his unique theory of "detached involvement."

Parikh, 72, narrates the origin of detached involvement in his book *Managing Your Self* (Blackwell Publishers, 1991). As a young MBA student at Harvard Business School, he was disturbed when the school dean admonished the students never to be content with whatever they *had* achieved because the moment they did so their drive for doing better would get dampened. This thinking went against the value system he had grown up with: "to try to experience during every moment of our existence the maximum possible satisfaction with whatever we have achieved."

There is, of course, an essential precondition, says Parikh: "We have to ensure that we have made the maximum possible effort toward achieving whatever goals we may have set for ourselves. But as far as the results are concerned, we have to accept them with equanimity, for such results depend on external variables over which we do not have full control." The key to success, he concludes, is drawing satisfaction from an inner sense of joy and not from the rewards or results one strives for in one's external environment. This is the essence of detached involvement.

In the following article, Parikh describes how detached involvement can transform professional and personal relationships into opportunities for growth.

What are the things that go wrong in your organization and your life? Chances are, every one of them is a result of a mismanaged relationship.

Now that service and individual talent are the true value added in any business, well-managed relationships with customers, suppliers, employees, and competitors become central to success. As the distinction between life inside and outside of work becomes increasingly blurred, so have our working relationships and life relationships become interchangeable.

The many threads of our relationships can be a prison in our lives or a cocoon for growth. Which will it be? We can choose growth if we know how to apply the proper concepts.

There has been such a torrent of new ideas—as seen in the proliferation of management concepts and self-help books—that we certainly do not lack useful ideas. However, most of us find it difficult to put them into practice.

## Our Inner Conflicts

The underlying issue is about changing our thinking from a reactive level to a proactive and creative level to enable us to convert our knowledge into behavior, leading to appropriate relationships. To achieve this, we need to overcome barriers to change.

The first barrier is the inner conflict we experience whenever we face change. On one hand, as a living system, we must grow and change. At the same time, we want to stay in our comfort zones and resist change.

Let's take the metaphor of a seed to overcome this paradox. Do we want to remain seeds, and feel secure in our comfort zones? Or do we want to have the courage to nurture the seed appropriately so that it can break open and blossom into a full-grown plant?

The second barrier is our ego-identity. If we identify ourselves with any beliefs, views, or values, it becomes difficult to change them, as that would imply destroying our very identity. This creates a barrier to change.

We generally tend to prove ourselves right rather than improve ourselves and, therefore, we need to detach and liberate ourselves from our belief systems. This freedom will in turn enhance the proactive courage we need to keep our minds open to a different level of thinking, feeling, and doing—making our relationships more meaningful and effective.

The key to transcending these barriers of change-resistance and ego-identity is *detached involvement*—an expanded level of consciousness, of relationship, of self-identity—that can bridge the gap between what we like to do, what we have to do, and what we are able to do.

Detached involvement enables us to deepen our relationship with our inner self. Paradoxical as it may seem, detachment leads to an expanded relationship with our self, and involvement from such an expanded self-relationship leads to a deeper and more authentic relationship with our inner body-mind-emotion dynamics with our ego sense. With such an expanded and deeper relationship within ourselves, we can begin to relate to our outer relationships with a more proactive and creative attitude.

## Pitfalls of Overattachment

Following are two analogies that explain the condition of detached involvement in more practical terms.

Consider your relationship to the chair you are sitting in. As long as you remain in it, can you observe the whole chair? Obviously not. To fully observe the chair, you need to get out of it.

But before you can consider the possibility of getting out of the chair, you will first have to accept intellectually that you only occupy the chair, you are not the chair. Once you accept this "relationship," you can detach yourself from the chair and observe it more fully.

In the process of observing the chair, something interesting is happening. When you are in the chair, not only can you not observe it fully, you also cannot move the chair or manage it! In fact, the chair, in a sense, manages you! Your entire physical posture is controlled or managed by the chair.

From this experience, we can distill the first law of human relationships: "You can never manage effectively *that* to which you are identified or attached. And whatever you are attached to or identified with manages you." Any object of addiction or over-attachment will always dominate and manage you.

This leads to the second law of human relationships: "You can relate to or manage far more effectively *that* person, object, event, or idea from which you are somewhat detached or not overly involved with."

Now, consider the way you hold the steering wheel of a car while driving. When you were still learning how to drive the car, you must have held the wheel tightly. There were so many variables to cope with while driving that, as a learner, you must have held on to the wheel tightly— an illusion of control! But once you had been driving for some time, how would you hold the wheel? Much more lightly, with mastery—a balanced "detached-involved" relationship with the wheel.

Let us continue with this analogy. Every car has a gearbox. Gears enable us to adjust the power of the engine and the speed of the car to suit external road conditions. While driving a car, if you want to shift the gear to another position, you have to pass through the neutral! Only when you are in the "neutral" (proactive) can you then go to any other gear-position of your choice; you cannot do so directly. It is the same case with our "response-ability" in dealing with relationships in a proactive and creative way—to develop win-win relationships.

Keeping these two analogies in mind will constantly remind us of the power of detached involvement: courageous and creative proactivity. To be proactive implies having the power to choose our responses in any situation. To be creative implies the ability to generate different possible responses. ■

---

Excerpted from **"Managing Relationships: Making a life while making a living"** by Jagdish Parikh (jparikh@cersite.com). © 1999 by the author. Published by Capstone Publishing Limited (www.capstone.co.uk), Oxford OX2 0JX, United Kingdom. Reprinted by permission of Capstone Publishing, 1999.

## Online Resources

- **Featured company**
  Centre for Executive Renewal
  http://www.cersite.com

- **Related articles**
  "Step Away From It!"
  By Jerry Hirshberg
  Every leader knows what to do when a project is falling behind schedule and
  the ideas aren't flowing: Get everyone to just hunker down. But sometimes,
  the best way of moving work forward is by not working at all.
  http://www.mgeneral.com/3-now/98-now/050998jh.htm

  "13 Ways to Save Time, Energy, and Money . . . Delegate!"
  How to become a master at delegation
  http://www.smartbiz.com/sbs/arts/ict1.htm

# The Mission of Enterprise

## Konosuke Matsushita

*Founder, Matsushita Electric Industrial Company Ltd.*
*Japan*

"Production aimed at enriching the life of every person on earth is the sacred mission of a manufacturer."

**Konosuke Matsushita**

Among the giants of Japanese business, the late Konosuke Matsushita stands out for a number of reasons. He was one of the central figures in the post-World War II Japanese economic miracle, having built a gigantic corporation with innovative management and marketing techniques. During his tenure, revenue growth at Matsushita Electric Industrial Company Ltd. grew by US$49.5 billion (in 1994 US dollars).

By the 1980s, the company Matsushita founded in 1918 had grown to an empire dominating the electronics and appliance fields under the brand names of Panasonic, Technics, and Quasar, the source of some 14,000 different products, from the original bicycle lamp to television sets to computer chips. It employed 120,000 people worldwide, with sales of more than US$40 billion a year. No wonder then that when Matsushita died in 1989, at the age of 94, the Japanese press canonized him as the "god of management."

Today, Matsushita Electric Industrial has sales of US$71.1 billion and employs almost 282,000 people worldwide. The company's growth has been attributed to what *Fortune* magazine describes as "a curious mix of capitalism and religion." Matsushita fervently believed that the ultimate aim of production was to eliminate poverty and create prosperity. So he raised production volume and went against conventional Japanese practices by lowering prices.

In this article, excerpted from his book *Quest for Prosperity: The Life of a Japanese Industrialist*, Matsushita describes how he conceived the mission of his enterprise.

B y the end of 1931, Matsushita Electric Industrial had four divisions—electric wiring fixtures, electrothermal devices, radios, and lamps and dry batteries—and was making more than

200 different types of products. As the depression wore on, this steady growth astounded people in the electric industry. The employees themselves were delighted with the undaunted way the company had ridden through the crisis and was steadily continuing its growth, and it aroused among them a strong sense of solidarity.

They say adversity makes a man wise, and how true that is. The depression had taught me a great deal and helped me to develop firm principles of personnel management. From that time on, the performance and caliber of our employees improved markedly.

The prospects for recovery of business in general and the electric industry in particular being much brighter, I was eager to put into practice my ideas for aggressive expansion of the company. Then, one day, one of our customers, whom I shall call Mr. U, came to call.

## An Invitation

Mr. U described to me the joys of religious faith that he discovered in his sect and invited me to visit their temple. But I was not ready to embrace the teachings of his sect immediately. So I thanked him for his invitation but declined it.

Still, Mr. U came back four or five times after that visit. On one such visit, he again invited me to visit their temple, not to decide whether or not to enter the faith, but just to see it for myself. Because of his eagerness and his repeated visits, I found it difficult to refuse his offer.

We set off one day, arriving at the head temple of Mr. U's sect in the early morning. He kept up a detailed running commentary as we went around. We proceeded first to the main hall of the temple. Its awesome size and the splendor of the architecture were made all the more impressive by the spotless cleanliness of the grounds.

Then we went on to the memorial hall of the founder of the sect, which was then under construction. A large building was taking shape, and I could see many people working there. Mr. U told me they were all followers of the sect who contributed their labor to the temple for free. Covered with sweat, they were working with great energy. I was amazed.

It was around noon when we finally descended to the foot of the hill. Finally, Mr. U said he wanted to take me to the lumber mill. The mill was situated on a spacious site and fully equipped with machines. Nearly 100 workers turned the timber donated daily in large quantities by followers from around the country into posts and beams.

Stepping inside, I could see many people laboring intently amid the roar of machines and the whine of huge saws. There was something solemn about the way they worked that created an atmosphere that made me instinctively straighten myself in respect. When I heard that almost all of the workers were followers of the sect, I understood.

The mill was the last place we saw that day, and I left feeling deeply moved. What I had witnessed was the power drawn forth by religion at work among men.

As our tour came to an end, I thanked Mr. U for a memorable day. We parted ways, and I made my way home by train.

**Religion and Management**

I found a seat on the train and began to think about the religion my friend had introduced me to. There was something to be learned from what I had seen—from the way it was thriving, from the energetic, dedicated way the members of the sect threw themselves into the construction work, and from the way everything worked with clockwork-like smoothness. It was the epitome of skillful management.

I began to think seriously about what true management ought to be like. I could not get the thought of religion on the one hand and management on the other off my mind. I stayed awake for a long time thinking about it. Religion was a holy pursuit aimed at guiding people out of suffering and toward happiness and peace of mind. My business, too, is sacred, I thought, in the sense that the ultimate aim of production is to wipe out poverty and create prosperity.

Eliminating poverty is a sacred task, the loftiest purpose in life. To achieve it, we must work hard and produce a great abundance of goods; this is our mission and our enterprise. Production aimed at enriching the life of every person on earth is the sacred mission of a manufacturer.

Not only spiritual peace but material abundance is necessary if the quality of human life is to be better and people are to be happier. Spiritual peace and material abundance are as inseparable as the two wheels of a cart. So, I realized, management of a religious organization and of a business concern are equally sacred and necessary pursuits.

I suddenly realized that my approach to business management had been all wrong. Business in general—and our enterprise in particular—is a holy mission that must prosper to an extent even greater than that of the religious sect I saw that day. And yet there were many companies in our industry that failed or whose operations were curtailed—all because of a mistaken approach to management. Failures in business are caused by self-centeredness, lack of righteousness, ignorance of the sacred mission of business, treating business as a shortsighted profit-making endeavor, and clinging to outmoded practices.

## Charting a New Course

The visit to the temple had made me realize that my management of Matsushita Electric Industrial until then had merely followed conventional commercial practices. I wanted to turn over a new leaf and begin running the company according to the true mission of enterprise immediately. I now knew the correct course for Matsushita Electric.

I mapped out a concrete plan for materializing the mission of our company as I now envisioned it. The plan provided a rough outline of how Matsushita Electric Industrial could fulfill its mission as well as specific principles to guide it over a period of 250 years.

I chose May 5, 1932 to announce the launching of the new company mission to my staff. All the office workers of Matsushita Electric Industrial gathered at ten o'clock on the morning of May 5, 1932 at the Osaka Central Electric Club auditorium. A total of 168 people were present. Everyone seemed a little nervous, wondering what on earth I was going to say about a "mission."

"I asked you to come because I would like to explain to you the important mission which I believe Matsushita Electric Industrial must assume as a member of the business community," I began. "I have called you here to explain this mission and ask you to cooperate with and share in my commitment to it."

I went on to outline our achievements as a company, starting 15 years earlier as a family enterprise. We now had more than 100 office staff and over 1,000 factory workers. Sales amounted to about 3 million yen per annum. I expressed my deep gratitude for the assiduous labors on the part of staff and employees that had made this growth possible.

After enumerating these achievements, I then presented a written declaration of our company mission, which read as follows:

"Our company, the Matsushita Electric Industrial Works, was founded in 1918. Through harmony and cooperation among all our staff and employees, it has continued steady growth ever since, and today it enjoys the respect and admiration of the whole industry. Our pioneering spirit is ever vigorous, and we look forward to a promising future. We bear a heavy responsibility to society.

The main purpose of production is to manufacture items of good quality for daily use in abundant supply, thereby enriching the quality of life for everyone, and it is to this goal that I am dedicated. Achieving this mission is the ultimate purpose of Matsushita Electric, and we will devote untiring energy to the realization of that goal. I ask you all to share in and understand this, and to do your best."

The change in the mood of the company following the declaration of our new mission was a remarkable phenomenon. Employee morale was excellent, and we realized that it would require strong leadership to keep it that way. Believing that there should be certain explanations of Matsushita business principles to outsiders and that the employees would need specific guidance to encourage them in their day-to-day activities, I set forth the following seven principles:

*Contribution to society.* We will conduct ourselves at all times in accordance with the Basic Management Objective, faithfully fulfilling our responsibilities as industrialists in the community in which we operate.

*Fairness and honesty.* We will be fair and honest in all our business dealings and in our personal conduct. No matter how talented or knowledgeable we may be, without personal integrity we can neither earn the respect of others nor enhance our own self-respect.

*Cooperation and team spirit.* We will pool our abilities to accomplish the goals that we share. No matter how skilled we are, without cooperation and team spirit, we will be a company in name only.

*Untiring effort for improvement.* We will constantly strive to improve our ability to contribute to society through our business activities. Only through such untiring effort can we fulfill our Basic Management Objective and help to realize lasting peace and prosperity.

*Courtesy and humility.* We will be cordial and modest, always respecting the rights and needs of others to strengthen healthy social relationships and improve the quality of life in our community.

*Adaptability.* We will continually adapt our thinking and behavior to the ever-changing conditions around us, taking care to always act in harmony with nature to ensure progress and success in our endeavor.

*Gratitude.* We will act out of a sense of gratitude for all the benefits we have received, confident that this attitude will be a source of boundless joy and vitality, enabling us to overcome any obstacles we encounter. ■

---

The biographical sketch was drawn using the following sources:

Katayama, Frederick H. "God of Management." *Fortune:* May 22, 1989.

Posey, Carl. "50 Years in Time: An Asian Edison Invents the New Japan, Electronics Titan Konosuke Matsushita Have Industry Its Philosophy." *Time:* November 25, 1996.

Pospisil, Vivian. "Matsushita Leadership: Lessons from the 20th Century's Most Remarkable Entrepreneur (book review)." *Industry Week:* April 21, 1997.

# Online Resources

- **Featured company**
  Matsushita Electric Industrial Co., Ltd.
  http://www.mei.co.jp

- **Related article**
  "Mission Statements Equal Profits"
  Research by *The Journal of Business Strategy* suggests that companies with mission statements are more likely to be profitable than those without. The article lists the common elements of mission statements covered in the study.
  http://www.smartbiz.com/sbs/arts/hph4.htm

- **Related Web site**
  PHP Institute, Inc.
  The think tank started by Konosuke Matsushita in 1946 has for its mission "to bring Peace, Happiness, and Prosperity (PHP) to the world." The institute is probably best known as one of Japan's most visible publishing houses, producing just under a dozen magazines and hundreds of books each year.
  http://www.php.co.jp/english.html

# Between the Transient and the Enduring

*Jaime Augusto Zobel de Ayala II*

President and CEO, Ayala Corporation
Philippines

"A strong, healthy, and profitable company does not sprout overnight, no matter how effective its managers."

**Jaime Augusto Zobel de Ayala II**

Ayala Corporation has been called an "aging battleship"—"slow to maneuver and cautious even in the calmest of economic seas." The Philippines' oldest and largest conglomerate, which runs major telecommunications, banking, and food businesses, has been known—and criticized—for its prudent financial management.

For example, while flashier competitors snapped up land and condominiums during the property boom of the early 1990s, saddling them with debt, Ayala Corp. stuck to its decades-old conservatism and kept its borrowing low. However, when the financial turmoil in the region put an end to the once-booming property market, its competitors found themselves deep in debt. Ayala Corp., on the other hand, had the cash to acquire properties at reduced prices.

A conservative financial approach is just one of the basic tenets which has helped Ayala Corp. weather storms for more than a century and a half, says president and CEO Jaime Augusto Zobel de Ayala II, widely known as "JAZA." In an article in the *Emerging Markets IMF/World Bank Daily*, JAZA credits his father, Jaime Zobel de Ayala, now chairman of Ayala Corp., for establishing the conglomerate's key strengths of decentralization and good management.

As a holding company, Ayala Corp. is organized into highly independent subsidiaries at the operating and financial levels. This structure allows the group excellent financial flexibility: with five listed companies in Ayala Corp., the conglomerate can raise money at different levels with a wide range of instruments.

Decentralization also allows room for creativity at the management level, helping engender good management. Though JAZA and his brother Fernando remain firmly in charge of the Ayala empire, they run the business not as a "murky family fiefdom" but as a transparent and professionally managed public company. Between 1992 and 1997, when the Philippine economy boomed and the Ayalas expanded into telecommunications and infrastructure, they beefed up their ranks with professional managers and gave them incentives such as stock options and merit-based promotions.

The 42-year-old JAZA, who took over the running of the group from his father in 1995, acknowledges that his family's legacy influenced the way he has shaped the US$2.6-billon company to meet the special needs of the late twentieth century. Under his leadership, the Ayala group of companies has grown 13% annually in revenue and has posted an annual return on equity over the last four years of 20%. In 1998, the group recorded nearly US$1 billion in revenues from businesses as diverse as real estate to retailing to information technology. The group's 1999 revenues were 34.5 billion pesos.

JAZA has certainly reaped the rewards of applying the enduring lessons of business. In this speech, which he delivered at the 1998 commencement exercises at the Asian Institute of Management, he cautions new managers against management fads and theories, and advises them to learn the really useful and lasting lessons of business life.

T his is a time when Asian managers—under the lash of the current crisis—have been humbled on many fronts. These days, many see Asian managers as the last persons to go to for sage advice on business management.

Asia's time of troubles, however, does not make the profession of management irrelevant. As you go through the corporate ruins and the adversities of the times, you will see again and again what happens when time-honored rules and principles are thrown out the window in the rush for profits. Besides, there are a number of Asian companies that have stood well under the gales of crisis.

I shall focus my remarks today on just one key point. And it is this: As you make your way in the world, practicing your profession, running a company or helping to run one, learn to distinguish between the *transient* and the *enduring* lessons of business life. And then apply the enduring truths to the hundred and one problems you will face as a professional manager and business leader.

As an executive who not so long ago was also in business school, I see the need, more than ever, for managers to get to the core truths because of the bewildering changes that have taken place and are now taking place in the world of business. I will cover these through three broad areas in my talk.

## Lessons from the Crisis

The first will cover the Asian crisis and its implications to all of us. The world is moving rapidly into what is popularly called the *new global economy*. In this new economy, products can be developed at a fraction of the time it took in the old economy, information is the most important resource, services and products are being custom-built to order, quality is dramatically improving, and costs are being driven down through the use of new technologies.

Secondly, I will cover the fact that the very discipline of management shifts between new fads and theories, and it is much harder now to distinguish between the really useful and the ephemeral in all this counsel from management gurus and consultants. I believe that unless we know what is really important, we managers could become more confused than enlightened.

Thirdly, I would like to expand on the fact that business success today comes in many forms. There is success that is achieved by cutting corners and straining the limits of both law and prudence. And there is success that comes from hard work, creativity, and values. I believe that business success that truly lasts rests on the straight rather than the crooked path.

Let me now go through each point and start with what we can learn from the Asian crisis. Asia today is a veritable school for business management. Tremendous change has occurred in Asia since June 1997 when Thailand devalued the baht. Since then, Asia has lived through a wrenching wake-up call.

Every corporate leader and manager will, of course, prefer to manage and lead during times of expansion and growth. Yet the greatest tests for management and leadership often come during times of crisis. To paraphrase the poet Rudyard Kipling, if your organization can keep its head above water while others are losing theirs, then you are managing things right.

If the Asian crisis were to produce a timidity and fearfulness among Asian managers, then it would truly prove to be catastrophic. It is a mistake to say that the Asian miracle was just a mirage. But it could become one if we Asians didn't quickly shake off the trauma. As someone once said, "The difference between a rut and a grave is the depth of the hole." Asia is just in a rut, and it would be best if we all understood this.

Similarly, if we took the wrong lessons away from the crisis—like the counsel for a return to protectionism and regulatory controls—the Asian miracle would indeed be over. Among the lessons managers must take to heart are:

- Rules are there for a reason, annoying though they may be. Asia ignored them to its sorrow, resulting in failed financial institutions and corporate bankruptcies. Transparency is a must for recovery and growth in the future.
- Democracy and markets do go together. The mantra of Asian values as an apology for authoritarian government has proved to be false.
- The right government policy is important, but it is finally private enterprise that must drive development. In the last analysis, it was the Asian enterprise, Asian management, and Asian labor that really fueled the Asian economic miracle. And they must fire up its revival.

Let me now move on to the second point of ephemeral fads and enduring realities. Distinguishing between the transient and the enduring is also necessary within the discipline of management itself. Our profession today is the prisoner of too many fads and theories. And many of us are at a loss to know which of these—if any—are truly useful or worthwhile.

We've been asked to tear down office doors so that employees and officers can have a greater sense of camaraderie. We have been urged to downsize, empower, delayer, and reengineer to improve the efficiency of our operations.

I do not doubt that each of these management theories has something to recommend it. What I worry about is losing sight of the harder thinking necessary to really succeed in business. Reengineering, for example, has been criticized for ignoring the human side of management and for sacrificing such intangible goods as commitment and creativity to short-term efficiency.

The truth is that real business success cannot be anchored on just a theory. As *The Economist* has observed, many of the world's best companies never bother with fads. The magazine reports: "These companies have the self-confidence to rely on their own judgment, and they have the common sense to realize that their problems are particular to them and cannot be treated with off-the-shelf remedies. 3M, for example, rejected new orthodoxy that a growing company should concentrate on one line of business. Hewlett-Packard ignored the teaching about earning curves and market shares."

## Living Companies

This brings me to my third point. Arie de Geus, a retired Royal Dutch/ Shell Group executive, calls successful companies that grow through generations "living companies" because they are comparable to living organisms, i.e., they adapt to their environment, and manage change effectively. He has distilled his thoughts in his book *Living Companies* (Harvard Business School Press, 1997).

De Geus points out that the striking thing about commercial corporations is that they are relative newcomers in the history of institutions in the world. And compared to religious, educational, political, and other social institutions, business corporations have a high mortality rate. Over the first five years of the 1990s, for instance, 143 companies disappeared from the Fortune 500 list.

But then there are a few companies that have shown great longevity, spanning centuries. These organizations "know who they are, and they understand how they fit into the world," writes de Geus. What are their secrets?

And the answer, I was surprised to discover from de Geus's empirical evidence, has nothing to do with anything fancy. It rests on common sense, prudence, and a sense of social responsibility. Living companies are sensitive to the environment, which enables them to learn and adapt; have cohesion and identity; practice tolerance and decentralization, which enables them to build constructive relationships with other entities, within and outside themselves; and have a strict policy of conservative financing, which enables them to govern their own growth and evolution effectively.

## Trust and Integrity

All this is to say that in the long run, companies must build on core principles and values. Within the context of de Geus's living companies are two important principles that we cannot overemphasize—the cultivation of integrity in the company and the building of trust within and outside it.

It is clear that the businesses that have survived through the years and grown to world-class status are those that have a clear ethical sense of who and what they are. They believe that success is achieved through hard work, diligence, honesty, and quality service and products for customers. And they are led and managed by boards and executives who are totally accountable to shareholders.

There is no question that truly successful companies—and truly successful management and leadership—are founded on a high degree of integrity. For it is through integrity that companies build trusts with its stockholders, its employees, and its publics.

High-trust organizations develop much faster than low-trust ones because of the power of shared values and social capital. As Warren Bennis, distinguished professor of business administration and founding chairman of The Leadership Institute at the University of Southern California, once said: "Trust is the emotional glue that binds followers and leaders together. It cannot be mandated or purchased, it must be earned. Trust is the basic ingredient of all organizations, the lubrication that maintains the organization."

Finally, I want to say something about the important relationship between technique and experience in business life. As managers and leaders, we rely on two kinds of learning in our work. There is the learning we get from business school about the nuts and bolts of running a business. And there is the learning we get from the university of experience of life.

Though I still consider myself young, I have done enough schooling in these two universities to realize that both are invaluable for the tasks of management in the real world. They complement each other. Business school provides us the discipline and the tools to structure the task, manage our time, and organize our companies effectively. The school of life provides us the vital links to one another and to society. It reminds us that a corporation is not an island unto itself; it has a responsibility to its employees, its public, and to the larger society.

To build organizations that last and fill a purpose in the economy and society, we cannot merely worship by the profit motive or the managerial fashions of the day. We must imbibe the enduring lessons of business life, integrate our efforts into those of the community as a whole, and earn the trust of all the publics we touch.

In a sense, the Asian crisis serves us well as a school in which to learn both old and new lessons. Adversity can shape Asian companies for the rigors of survival and competition in the world. For whichever way the world may turn under globalization and the pervasive rearrangement of structures and beliefs, certain truths will always endure.

As you all go back to the real world, remember the difference between the transient and the enduring. A strong, healthy, and profitable company does not sprout overnight, no matter how effective its managers. It evolves like a living organism. It grows because it has a firm sense of identity and purpose, it is rooted in core principles and values, and it nurtures an active regard for the welfare of its people and the community around it. ■

---

The biographical sketch was drawn using the following sources:

"Leaders for the Millennium: Business and Finance." *Asiaweek:* June 11, 1999.

Chowdhury, Neel. "Is the Asian Conglomerate Doomed?" *Fortune:* April 12, 1999.

Tierney, Jennifer. "Emerging Markets CEO of the Year." *Emerging Markets IMF/World Bank Daily:* October 5, 1998.

Tiglao, Rigoberto. "Hamburger Heaven." *Far Eastern Economic Review:* December 31, 1998 and January 7, 1999.

Tiglao, Rigoberto. "Steady as She Grows." *Far Eastern Economic Review:* December 25, 1997 and January 1, 1998.

## Online Resources

- **Featured companies**
  Asian Institute of Management
  http://www.aim.edu.ph

  Ayala Corporation
  http://www.ayala-group.com

  Hewlett-Packard Company
  http://www.hp.com

  Minnesota Mining and Manufacturing Company (3M)
  http://www.mmm.com

- **Related articles**
  "Conglomerates in Emerging Markets: Tigers or Dinosaurs?"
  By Zafer Achi, Chipper Boulas, Ian Buchanan, Jorge H. Forteza, and Lando Zappei
  Blamed for many of Asia's economic woes, conglomerates are still viable, if they employ any of three strategies well.
  http://www.strategy-business.com/policy/98206/

  "Why Ideas Matter"
  By Nan Stone and Joan Magretta
  Executives will always need new ideas, not because they are addicted to fads, but because the business environment is dynamic and continually throws new challenges their way.
  http://www.ac.com/ideas/Outlook/6.99/over_ideas.html

# Rules for Revolutionaries

## Guy Kawasaki

*CEO, Garage.com*
*United States*

"Life for a revolutionary is all about kicking 'but': 'You have an interesting product but . . . 'I can see where there needs to be a better way, but . . .' 'I'd like to help you, but . . .' "

**Guy Kawasaki**

When Garage.com, the Internet matching service for entrepreneurs and investors founded by CEO Guy Kawasaki, opened in 1998, the A-list of entrepreneurs, venture capitalists, and media people who showed up at the launch party got free massages, their pictures on mock covers of *Forbes* magazine, and raffles for a one-year lease on a Mercedes. Only Kawasaki, a 45-year-old columnist, speaker, and high-tech marketing pioneer, would have the go-for-broke attitude to pull off a media stunt like that. As a result, the Silicon Valley-based firm was written up in the major dailies and just about every tech-savvy media publication around.

How can Kawasaki, who won his notoriety through what he calls "fanatical devotion to a troubled revolutionary company (Apple Computer)", write *Rules for Revolutionaries*, a book about creating successful revolutions? With trademark irreverence, he cites two reasons in his foreword: "Short answer: Chutzpah. Long answer: The best possible credential for the author of this book is scar tissue from battling resistance to change."

In this article, Kawasaki discusses some of the different rules anyone taking on the establishment has to play by.

## Think Different

Think different to change the rules. By definition, if you don't change the rules, you aren't a revolutionary, and if you don't think different, you won't change the rules.

In 1955, the Walt Disney Company opened Disneyland and set the standard of showmanship, efficiency, and profitability for the amusement park business. Before Disneyland, the rule was that amusement parks needed big, scary roller coasters to succeed. Disneyland changed all that by featuring *theme* rides instead of *thrill* rides. For the next 30 years, amusement park companies played by Disney's rules, or they hardly mattered at all.

Then along came Jay Stein. Stein ran MCA Recreation, the company that owns Universal Studios. Universal Studios was an also-ran in the amusement park business because it merely re-purposed content from the studio's main business of making movies. The rule it played by was simple and stupid: Stuff people on a tram, take them "behind the scenes" of a movie, drop them off, and hope they buy souvenirs.

But when MCA built Universal Studios Florida, Stein threw out his own company's standard operating procedures. Instead of "See how we make movies," his pitch became "Come ride the movies." *Back to the Future* (the movie) became *Back to the Future* (the ride). Stein combined theme and thrill to rewrite Universal's rules.

He then went after the de facto ruled established by Disney: Be nice, gentle, and politically correct. For example, the bleeding edge of Disneyland's rides is attractions like the Haunted Mansion and the Pirates of the Caribbean. They are works of art—far more "multimedia" than the vaunted multimedia efforts of the computer business—but not exactly risky.

Stein decides that rides wouldn't be nice—instead, they would kick people's butts. So at Universal Studios Florida there are blood, guts, flames, and explosions. Every day there are customer complaints that the fireballs are too hot. The shark in the *Jaws* ride comes so close to the boat that it will break people's arms if they are dumb enough to put them in harm's way. And every day, thousands of people come back for more.

There's not much that Disney can do about this full-frontal attack, because it is a prisoner of its own fun-but-safe standards and image. Stein turned the strengths of Disney into a constraining weakness. If Disney tried to live up to its rides, it would lose its core audience and blur its image.

**Cross the Chasm**

You've shipped. Initial sales are good. Now get ready to fall into the Chasm.

Credit Geoffrey Moore for this concept. In his book, *Crossing the Chasm*, Moore defines the Chasm "as a significant gulf that exists between the market made up of early adopters, and the markets of more pragmatic buyers."

Early buyers are completely different from other buyers, so crossing the Chasm requires breaking down the barriers that prevent widespread trial and then dominating niche markets where your products have attained success. If you dominate enough niche markets, your product will achieve critical mass and become a "no brainer" to buy.

At the start of a revolution, five kinds of barriers prevent adoption: ignorance, inertia, complexity, channel, and price.

Reducing ignorance involves making people aware of a new product or service. If the world doesn't know that you've built a better mousetrap, it certainly won't beat a path to your door.

Inertia is usually the most challenging and frustrating barrier. It arises after people know there is a better way but still won't adopt it. It can be a crushing experience when you learn firsthand that most of the world doesn't care if there is a better mousetrap even after they hear about it.

The complexity barrier is the difficulty of using a product. No matter how revolutionary your mousetrap, if it takes a whole day or a Ph.D. to set it up, it won't succeed.

Resistance of the distribution channel to sell and support your product can be deadly. This requires fixing the old channel—but this is usually quite difficult because of its inherent preference for the status quo. It may be easier to create a new channel instead.

"Price" is the scariest word to a revolutionary. On one hand, you should get as much money as possible from early adopters because they derive the most value from it. And you need their money to sustain churning. On the other, if your price eliminates consideration from early adopters, you'll never get to—much less cross—the Chasm.

Following are some ways to break down barriers.

*Enable test-driving.* Enabling people to test-drive your product or service is a powerful way to lower barriers to adoption. For example, the WD-40 Company created great awareness of the product by giving away thousands of samples to soldiers in the Vietnam War as a way to keep their weapons clean in the tropical climate. When these soldiers returned home, they wanted the product for civilian uses.

A more peaceful example of test-driving is how Revlon provided fingernail-shaped paper samples of its LavenDare line of nail polish. The samples had sticky backs that enable people to place them on their fingernails to see how they like the colors.

*Create a sense of ownership.* People don't erect barriers to the adoption of a product in which they have a sense of ownership, that is, a psychological bond with a product someone helped design.

I've done this several times when designing software. Journalists and reviewers gave me feedback about how to change a piece of software, and assuming I could convince the programmer, I tried to accommodate their suggestions. Making this change flattered them and reduced the likelihood that they would pan a product that they "designed."

Bottom line: Determine who is likely to erect barriers and get them to help you to refine your product or service. They may have ideas to significantly improve it. Even if they don't, they are a lot less likely to try to prevent its adoption.

*Make Matterhorns out of mountains.* This is a page out of the recommendations of a marketing firm in Silicon Valley named Regis McKenna, Inc. It recommends that you make a Matterhorn out of a mountain by positioning a revolutionary product or service "outrageously."

Outrageous positioning is intended to shock people into recognizing the potential impact of your product or service—thus, it is meant to reduce the ignorance and inertia barriers. Some examples follow:

- Product/Service: Bose AM/FM Radio
  Outrageous Positioning: Listening to this radio is better than being at the concert hall.

- Product/Service: Silicon Graphics Workstation
  Outrageous Positioning: Anyone can make movies as well as George
  Lucas with this computer.
- Product/Service: Southwest Airlines
  Outrageous Positioning: Cheaper and faster than driving.

Not every company can use this tactic. There has to be an element
of truth to your claim, and your company needs to have a solid
reputation. If you break down the barriers and delight many customers,
then your product or service will become the safe buy. You've made it
across the Chasm.

## Eat Like a Bird, Poop Like an Elephant

If someone tells you that you eat like a bird, the implication is that you
don't eat much. Yet for their body weight, birds eat a lot. The peripatetic
hummingbird, for example, eats the equivalent of 50% of its weight
every day.

Chances are that no one will tell you that you poop like an elephant,
because elephants poop 165 pounds per day. However, there are two
serious messages for revolutionaries in these biological facts.

First, a successful revolutionary relentlessly searches for and absorbs
knowledge about the industry, customers, and competition. You do this by
pressing the flesh of your customers, attending seminars and trade shows,
reading journals, and browsing the Internet.

Second, you need to spread the large amount of information knowledge
that you've gained. This means sharing information with your fellow
employees and occasionally even with your competitors.

The Japanese have a saying that the more important a function, the
more you should use amateurs. Nothing is more important than gathering
information about your customers and your competition, so you should
never leave it to marketing research professionals.

Honda has real-world market research all figured out. It uses the *sangen*
or "three actuals" approach: actual product, actual person, and actual

situation. Here are some real-world examples from other companies:

- Actual product. After it opened, Walt Disney spent every weekend at Disneyland. He would slip into shows and rides unseen, then offer his critique. He was experiencing the same product as customers.
- Actual person. During the Korean War, Kelly Johnson, the leader of the Skunk Works group at Lockheed, took a tour of the Korean battlefront. He traveled over 23,000 miles and visited 15 air bases to learn firsthand what improvement pilots wanted in their planes.
- Actual situation. Alfred Sloan used to take off from General Motors headquarters once per quarter and spend a week selling cars, working in a parts operation, or doing something at a dealership.

Here are the four things you need to do to spread (and receive) information in the most efficient ways:

*Get over the paranoia.* Stop worrying about the negative effects of spreading information to other parts of your company as well as colleagues and competitors. Sure, be judicious about what you share, but err on the side of sharing too much.

*Make it simple, correct, and frequent.* Spread efficiently by making the information you're sharing simple and correct; and do the spreading often. The better and more frequent the information that you provide, the better and more frequent the information you'll get back.

*Use the Web!* Before Internet, spreading information had large costs: printing, travel, entertaining, and long-distance telephone charges. Today, the Web has reduced these costs and made information available around the world.

*Get all levels involved.* Information spreading, like pressing flesh, needs to be democratized and institutionalized. Enable all parts of your company to share in their special knowledge whether the function is research or copyright law. ∎

---

The biographical sketch was drawn using the following source:

"How Garage.com Set Off So Much Buzz." *Business Week*: November 24, 1998.

## Online Resources

- **Featured companies**
  Garage.com
  http://www.garage.com

  MCA Recreation
  http://www.mca.com

  Regis McKenna, Inc.
  http://www.mckenna-group.com

- **Related articles**
  "Idea Summit"
  By Anna Muoio
  Rolf Smith has spent a career thinking about how people think. Now, he is helping people at some of the world's most powerful organizations to generate big ideas—and to rethink their whole approach to creativity.
  http://www.fastcompany.com/online/31/smith.html

  "Introducing New Products"
  By Michael T. Brandt
  Why do so many new products fail? Usually, for many reasons. This article reviews several of the critical issues that affect product introductions.
  http://www.inc.com/articles/details/0,3532,ART17958_CNT56,00.html

# Reengineering Your Life

## Chung Po-Yang

*Co-founder and Chairman Emeritus, DHL International Ltd.*
*Hong Kong SAR*

"Unlike a company, where one can declare bankruptcy and start over again, we can't live our lives all over again. How, then, do we get a new start?"

**Chung Po-Yang**

In 1972, Adrian Dalsey, a co-founder of what was then a fledgling U.S. courier company called DHL Airways Inc., visited Chung Po-Yang (widely known as "Po Chung"), an operations manager for an American company that was making toys in Hong Kong. Dalsey was only trying to do business with the company that Chung was working for. Little did he know that that fateful meeting would result in his gaining an enterprising associate.

Two days after they met, Chung resigned from his job and began to carve a niche as one of the world's leading package-delivery entrepreneurs with his co-founding of DHL International Ltd. The two separate DHLs—which make up DHL Worldwide Express, the world's largest international express delivery company—work together in what *Fortune* magazine calls "an unusual cooperative agreement." Chung delivers everything that the American DHL sends overseas, and the U.S. company handles packages that arrive in the U.S. from Chung's company—with no money changing hands.

Chung, 58, has described himself as a Taoist manager, following the Chinese philosophy of Taoism, which advocates minimal government. In "DHL's Management Philosophy and the Philosophy's Contribution to the Company's Global Success," a speech which he has delivered to many groups throughout the world, he identifies the three key philosophies that contribute to the "DHL company culture":

*Decentralization.* DHL's global system is never at rest; thousands of key decisions are being made round the clock, says Chung. Yet DHL's managers sleep well at night because employees on the spot, who master a wide range of varying regulations for moving shipments across borders, are empowered to make decisions.

*Strategic thinking at all levels of management.* At DHL, decision-making is pushed to the lowest level, and fast-track supervisors and assistant managers are trained to think strategically.

*An Asian family attitude.* Chung believes that a company which shows care and respect to its employees can expect its employees to reciprocate by showing loyalty, commitment, and diligence.

Chung is known for his humanist ideals. In this article, adapted from a speech which he delivered before members of the Young Presidents' Organization in Hong Kong in 1998, he explains how we can apply a four-step "mental and emotional reengineering process" to live happier, more productive lives.

C an we use business practices to better manage our lives, live them with more purpose, and increase our happiness? I believe we can, and would like to propose a new mental model that I have been working on.

My model is premised on the following:

Life can be looked at as a business: it has clients, products, and services; it has product quality standards; and it has profits and losses.

When businesses fail, they can declare bankruptcy and start over again. While human beings can't literally start afresh, they can undertake "mental and emotional reengineering" to ensure a high level of quality service, happiness, and self-esteem.

Business planning, which used to be short-term and reactionary, has become proactive and systematic. The same logic can be applied to life planning.

**The Business of Living**

These days, it is common for corporations to ask themselves what business they are in. To define life in business terms, we must ask ourselves the same basic questions that businesses ask: What am I here for? What is my purpose?

My definition of the business of an individual is as follows: *Each of us is an operating entity who has social contracts to provide service to all of the people with whom we come into contact and to receive service from them.*

From the moment of birth, when we first received service from our mothers, the doctors, and the nurses, until the time we die and receive service from the gravediggers, we are in a constant transaction service network with all of the people with whom we come into contact.

This definition requires us to judge the success of our life in terms of the service successes and failures that we have in our interactions with others, our customers, and clients. We use our personal evaluation of these interactions with other people to derive our personal service quality records. Our positive and negative evaluation of our service quality directly affects our sense of happiness, our peace of mind, and ultimately our self-esteem.

When we view our lives as an operating entity, we will see that many important aspects of business have counterparts in our personal lives. A business's customers correspond to our family, friends, and associates. Its corporate culture equals our personal philosophies. Its product or service equals our professional or personal services. A company's strategic plans correspond to our personal plans.

In a service business, service quality performance records, profit and loss statements, and balance sheets reflect the state of the business. There are similar records that reflect the state of one's life: "service quality records" are reflected in the accomplishments we are proud of; "profit and loss" can be measured as a sense of happiness and peace of mind; and a "balance sheet" is comparable to one's level of self-esteem.

Our profit and loss account can be interpreted as the net sum of our accumulated positive emotional scores over our negative emotional scores for a given period of time. While a business uses product quality, corporate morale, and dollar profits to measure its success, a human being uses accomplishments which he or she is proud of, peace of mind, and the feelings of contentment resulting from high self-esteem to measure his or her level of fulfillment and happiness.

Both in the business world and in the business of living, I believe there is a strong correlation between the quality of service and the level of happiness. I have put this belief into what I call Po Chung's Theorem: *Level of personal quality = Level of personal happiness.*

When a person starts to provide poor service, he or she begins to expect to receive poor service. After a while, once seemingly, small insignificant service quality losses will mount up and wipe out any accumulated capital on the emotional balance sheet. The end result is emotional bankruptcy and low self-esteem.

## Mental and Emotional Reengineering

Unlike a company, where one can declare bankruptcy and start over again, we know that we can't live our lives all over again. How, then, do we get a new start?

I believe we can begin by putting our own houses in order. In my case, I took an exhaustive inventory of my life and then systematically threw out all of my service failure records—all the mental baggage that was negatively affecting the service I was giving and receiving from my customers, including my live-in client.

But I knew that cleaning my house was not enough. I also needed to keep my house in order, that is, I would need to maintain a high level of service quality. I decided to design a strategy for the whole process. My four-step mental and emotional reengineering process is the result of this work.

1) *Take a full inventory of your positive and negative emotions.* I began by making two columns, one for accomplishments and good stories and another for service failures and bad stories. The reason I did this was very "businesslike." To know the state of a business, we prepare a spreadsheet of the service successes and failures. I did the same thing.

Taking a complete inventory helps you put your abstract thoughts into words. Sometimes, the simple act of writing down what had always been fleeting clarifies the problem or may even make it go away. You may even notice that your list of significant negative emotions is a lot shorter than you imagined it would be.

Also, putting a handle on each event makes it easier to manage. It amazed me just how few events and emotions really dominated my life. I found that the numbers were very manageable.

The most important aspect of making a personal inventory is honesty. You must not try to deceive your live-in client. Accept that these emotions are all water under the bridge. Kick yourself only once. Instead of saying, "if only I hadn't done that," say, "next time I will do this."

2) *Get rid of negative emotions.* Next, I visualized my emotional experiences as fishes. The positive emotions became goldfish; the negative emotions became black catfish. Putting these emotional experiences down on paper was like putting the goldfish and the catfish into an aquarium. I left the positive goldfish emotions in the aquarium where I could enjoy them. I took the catfish out and put them into a bucket where I could catch them easily and start killing them.

The process of taking inventory is not difficult, but it is tedious. You don't have to do it all in a day. You can set your own pace. You can kill a catfish every day, or you can have a mass execution in a weekend.

Dealing openly and honestly with each negative emotion and event, on paper, in writing, let me decide where and how to chop my catfish. Some catfish got chopped once. Others got minced. Eventually, I killed them all.

This process allowed me to make decisions that effectively gave me the power to reengineer my mission in life and the will to realign my lifestyle to correspond with my basic value system.

3) *Draw a blueprint for a purposeful life.* I started to reengineer my life and to repack my bags. I decided where I wanted to go and what I needed to take with me.

After taking an inventory and cleaning your house of negative emotions, the next step is to start writing a business plan. The typical headings of a business plan correspond to headings in a personal plan. For example: "mission statement" corresponds to "life goal"; "critical success factors" corresponds to "strengths and weaknesses"; "company summary" corresponds to "curriculum vitae"; and "market positioning" corresponds to "life philosophy."

4) *Monitor and ensure high-quality service.* One of the most important elements required to achieve the mission of a business is to

ensure high-quality service by installing a quality assurance process. I use daily or semi-weekly journal writing to carry out my own quality audit.

If you don't keep a journal, I suggest you start. In addition to reviewing your service record on a daily basis, you can gain other benefits from journal writing. You will develop the habits of having quiet time for yourself and systematically thinking emotional issues through. And you will have a record so you can monitor changes in your positions on issues over time.

Writing in my journal has allowed me to become better educated about myself and my higher-order needs. I have learned to reduce stress and anxiety, to be in better control of my emotions, and to identify the things that really contribute to my happiness and self-fulfillment.

In my journey of self-discovery, I learned that if I put a little effort into managing the routines and customer service aspects of my life, using a systematic and scientific method, I had more free time and the emotional freedom to live my life more artistically, creatively, and purposefully.

## Who's in Charge of Your Life?

Most businesses are built by owner-entrepreneurs. In the early stages of their development, the way each business is developed reflects the individual personality and philosophy of the owner-entrepreneur. We see this style nowadays in the "mom and pop" store or business.

One hundred years ago, this was also the way the industrial companies were managed in their infancies. Reactionary styles of management were the rule of the day. While such companies remained small, all business planning could be done and kept in the owner's head.

Today, management is proactive and knowledgeable. Successful companies have a clear sense of purpose and produce predictable results. Because a clear vision and business plan exist, the owner of a large corporation can retire or die without causing any major disruption of operations. The evolution of the business plan documents a shift from reactive business management to proactive business planning characterized by clearly defined business goals and strategies.

Looking at the business of life, I think it's possible to establish a similar rationale for taking the time to write a personal business plan for living our lives. In the past, people lived their lives like a mom and pop store— they made only short-term plans, and their important decisions were mostly reactive. But change is in the air. Visit any bookstore and you will find shelves full of self-improvement books.

Why are so many people interested in changing the way they live their lives? Most answers stem from these simple facts:

- Our basic needs are met. As a result, we don't need to spend as much time finding our next meal or looking after our shelter.
- We have more educational resources. Advanced education is available for everyone.
- We have greater mobility. Eighty days around the world has been reduced to less than 80 hours.
- We have higher fulfillment goals.
- We live much longer and we want much more out of our older years than to just eat and lie around in lounge chairs at a retirement home.

Given the circumstances, I think it's reasonable to ask ourselves, "Will we run our lives or will our lives run us?" If you want to spend the rest of your life as a mom and pop store, fine. If you want to live a proactive and managed life, it's not too late to get started. ■

---

# Online Resources

- **Featured company**
DHL Worldwide Express
http://www.dhl.com

- **Related articles**
"Life in the Balance"
By Dr. Irvin D. Yalom, with Ben Yalom
How can you find a balance between your professional and personal lives? The story of a workaholic CEO who couldn't address his personal problems until his professional career came to an end.
http://www.inc.com/incmagazine/archives/02980291.html

  "Making Waves"
By Tony Schwartz
Want to avoid burnout and increase your productivity? Sports psychologist Jim Loehr offers a unique approach to the challenge of optimizing performance.
http://www.fastcompany.com/online/28/tschwartz.html

# PART 2

# INSTILLING CORPORATE CULTURE

# McKinsey's Value Chain

## Rajat Gupta

### Managing Director, McKinsey & Company
### United States

"We don't manage our growth. It is the result of hundreds of different decisions made by all our cells."

**Rajat Gupta**

To hear CEO Rajat Gupta tell it, if you sat through a board meeting at McKinsey & Co., you'd never think this was the leading management consultancy firm. "Everybody's complaining about something we're not doing right, and it's not relative to our competitors, it's relative to our own aspirations," Gupta says in an interview.

McKinsey, although not the oldest and biggest management firm, is referred to as The Firm by those in the know. Through its consultants, which have helped to reshape virtually every big firm in the world, it wields extraordinary influence. McKinsey alumni, which include management author Tom Peters, have run institutions as varied as American Express, Ben & Jerry's, and the Confederation of British Industry.

The 8,500-employee firm, with 75 offices worldwide and revenues of US$2 billion, is known for its powerful collective ethos and legendary collegiality. This is a corporate culture which the 53-year-old Gupta, a McKinsey man for the past 27 years, has upheld.

Gupta believes the firm's premium on meritocracy played a part in his rise to the top. McKinsey follows a ruthless "up-or-out" policy: If you don't make it to the next level within a certain number of years, you are expected to leave. Associates, the new recruits, usually take about six years to become principals; about one in six makes it. It takes another six years to become a director, and only one in ten associates becomes one.

Gupta survived this cutthroat environment to become the firm's first India-born managing director. In this interview, he defines what makes for effective leadership and what lies behind the so-called McKinsey mystique.

In an increasingly competitive and uncertain global business environment, what makes for effective leadership? I think one of the things that is clear is that in this kind of dramatic change you'll see an even greater dispersion of performance, even in the same industry, so to really stay on top, you've got to do a lot more things simultaneously. Companies have to have that capability, either invested in a single individual or collectively at the top.

There's no question that the role of being a strategic architect on a global scale is increasingly important. The economics of almost every industry, not just the high-tech but the traditional industries, are dramatically changing as a result of globalization, deregulation, and technology. That creates an extraordinary set of opportunities for those who are strategically nimble.

I think there is a premium for that kind of strategic thinking in today's world. That is not to say that execution is unimportant. I think you have to simultaneously deliver on both the strategic position as well as on performance-based execution of strategies.

Another thing that is obvious is that there are going to be a number of different strategies that will be successful within the same industries. There are large integrated players who are providing, in a way, one-stop shopping—such as in financial services. At the same time, there will be players who will build terrific value propositions on a more defined slice of the business system and do it globally. And this is just two generic strategies—there are others. But you have to choose, you can't go from one strategy to the other. There has to be some staying power over time to a particular strategy.

So what you see in terms of CEO profiles is, first and foremost, extraordinarily good strategic thinkers who understand the changing nature of the industry structure and are shaping it themselves with their own moves. And at the same time there is still a strong premium on outstanding execution, and that will continue to pay rich dividends.

If these are two important dimensions, then you do also have the dimension of external communication. There are a lot of broad constituencies as a company functions on a multi-country, global basis.

Capital markets are extremely demanding. They want transparency, they want to know what's going on. And delivering results—the transparency of that to the marketplace—is more important today than ever before.

Another important aspect of the CEO profile and job is that of winning the war for talent. Attracting the best people gets tougher and tougher, and there is an extraordinary demand for high-quality people in every industry. You have to have the ability to retain outstanding talent. Ultimately that is a part of the CEO's responsibility.

## How Does a Company Create Leaders?

This is a question that is dear to our hearts. Because one of the noble purposes of the firm is to actually train business leaders, not only to be leading this firm, but businesses outside. And we consider that to be our contribution to the business world.

On our commitment to leadership development, I would say that there are at least three dimensions: two are vitally important and one probably somewhat less important. The formal training program gets talked about a lot, but I say that it is the least important in some ways. It's an extensive program, right from the day you join, and it goes from skill training to functional training to substantive ideas to broad leadership training. We invest a lot in that and it certainly has a role to play in leadership development.

But the two most important things, I believe, are, one, the whole notion of apprenticeship and mentoring, and the other, what I would call entrepreneurial space. The former refers to what you learn by observation, from doing together with someone who's done it before. Everything we do has a vertical team—people who've just joined, people who've been here for three or four years, people who've been here for 25 years. You learn by the interaction between the different experience levels in the firm. That's an ongoing process that I think is vital to leadership development.

The other aspect is somewhat opposite to this, which is that you learn a lot when you're thrown into a situation and you don't have a lot of help. You have a lot of entrepreneurial space in the sense that you have to improvise and learn very fast from your mistakes. I would hope that in anybody's career you would get an intensive apprenticeship experience for some of the time and an intensive entrepreneurial space where the fear of failing and learning from doing is the dominant form of learning. If you get a mixture of both, I think it goes a long way in truly developing you as a leader.

## Leveraging an Individual's Unique Talents While Fostering a Corporate Culture

We've done a lot of thinking on knowledge management. We see a level of knowledge which is embodied in individuals and that is important to any enterprise as they bring that knowledge to bear on what they do.

But there is something beyond that, a sort of collective knowledge of the enterprise, and that is much more than the sum of any individual knowledge. You see that in terms of a fundamental skill base that is developed in, say, customer service in a particular institution, or product innovation. This sort of collective knowledge is going to continue to be important and is going to be a source of distinctive advantage to enterprises.

The key here is to allow a lot of individual creativity and personal freedom within the culture. At McKinsey, we see that all the time. While we have an extremely strong culture, we are a cellular organization. You can form different cells, and they are extremely permeable. I can go in with three colleagues and say I want to start a project in this particular area in knowledge development or I want to go to a geography and start a practice.

There is great incentive for entrepreneurs to build networks that help make each of these cells successful. But this is not in any way to undermine the need for a culture, the need for a strong set of values with which we govern ourselves. I'm not particularly enamoured of a free-for-all type of attitude.

## Winning the War for Talent

If you look at the growth in the top-quality MBA programs and the growth in the market for talent, they're not quite proportional. So we have to work harder at attracting the best talent at the business schools, and at the same time, it's wise for us to diversify our sources of talent.

Business schools don't have a monopoly on talent in the world, and we find that there are many other sources. We were actually the first to have an extensive program in this and now our program of non-business school recruitment—Ph.Ds in economics and physics and all kinds of backgrounds—is bigger than the MBA recruitment program. And we feel comfortable in being able to quickly bring them up to speed on business ideas and concepts. We find that this is a better thing to do than reach deeper into business school recruiting, which has a danger of diluting quality.

It is true that the profession overall is supply-constrained, not demand-constrained, but we impose a certain cap on our supply. In a profession like ours, which is still largely apprentice-based and has a team-based approach, there is only so much growth you can have with quality. I've been with the firm 25 years and we've grown pretty much between 10% and 15% every year, no more, no less. It's not a managed number but it's sort of the natural consequence of paying attention to quality, to the apprentice nature of building up capabilities. And I'm quite happy with that.

## What Lies Behind the McKinsey Mystique?

Well, there are two or three things. Firstly, it's a value-led organization. We do absolutely put client interests first, we have a strong sense of partnership and collaboration, we have a participative form of governance and a commitment to meritocracy. You take those things and if you live them every day, you build a unique environment.

We are also never entirely satisfied. If you sat through a board meeting at McKinsey, you'd never think this was the leading management consultancy firm. Everybody's complaining about something we're not doing right, and it's not relative to our competitors, it's relative to our own aspirations. And there is a kind of generational contract that you have an obligation to leave the firm better than you found it, and we're constantly striving to live up to it.

For example, in the last two years we made an effort to think about the firm through the next decade. We had a task force made up of about 70 or 80 partners, working for 18 months, involving every partner in the firm. That's an extraordinary commitment to have this kind of dialogue. Now the traditional way to look at strategy would have been: "What would give us a differentiated service line?" "How can we be better than our competitors in what we offer?" and things like that. An equally valid and probably more interesting perspective to us would be "What do our clients need?" and "Can we provide a unique value proposition?"

But probably the most important one, which is not normally a strategy dimension that most firms would consider, is what are the aspirations of our partnership? What do they want to be? There are a lot of things that meet the first two tests, for example, that we don't want to be. So we define our strategy as 50% aspiration-based, 40% client-need-based, and 10% competitive-based.

In terms of attracting people, I would say that it fundamentally has to do with meritocracy. When you talk to McKinsey alumni, they always talk about the values and the commitment to developing people. You always leave a better professional than when you entered.

I have discussions with our partners all the time because they get a lot of offers. And the first question I always ask is, what is in their best interests? Because I think that if somebody gets an opportunity outside and it's in their best interests to be outside McKinsey, I look at our larger purpose to build leaders, whether they're effective in the organization or they're effective somewhere outside.

So it's those kinds of values. It's not a commercially driven firm. I must spend an hour a month looking at our financials. It is value-driven, people-driven, client-interest-driven. That's why we are able to maintain what I believe is a unique institution. It does get tougher and tougher to maintain in light of the size and the diversity, but I think we're quite competitive in doing it. ∎

---

Condensed from **World Link** (www.worldlink.co.uk), September/October 1998. © 1998 by World Link Publications Ltd., London EC4 5EX, UK. All rights reserved.

The biographical sketch was drawn using the following sources:
"Everything in the Garden's Lovely." *The Economist*: July 27, 1996.
Sreenivisan, Sreenath. "The Superboss." *Business Today:* April 22, 1994.

## Online Resources

- **Featured company**
  McKinsey & Company
  http://www.mckinsey.com

- **Related articles**
  "Brilliant Strategy, But Can You Execute?"
  By Claudio Aspesi and Dev Vardhan
  The best strategy for any company is a strategy it can implement. Before you choose one, think about what your company already does well. The experience of two industries—energy and pharmaceuticals—illustrates a new way to assess the fit between corporate strategy and corporate strengths.
  http://mckinseyquarterly.com/article_page.asp?articlenum=318

  "Develop Your Bench Strength!"
  By David A. Heenan and Warren Bennis
  The untimely death in 1997 of Coca-Cola CEO Roberto Goizueta reminded the world that no complex organization could afford to rely too heavily on a single leader, however gifted. Every organization needs the deep leadership provided by great co-leaders.
  http://www.mgeneral.com/3-now/99-now/072899dh.htm

# The Acer Way

## Stan Shih

*Founder and Chairman, Acer Group*
*Taiwan*

"Acer's 'fast-food business model,' 'client-server' structure, and 'global brand, local touch' strategies are the prescriptions which have enabled it to grow."

**Stan Shih**

Ask Acer Group chairman Stan Shih how he chose his company's name and chances are he'll say that *acer* (Latin for "spirited," "energetic") is short, easy to pronounce and, best of all, would appear near the top when companies are listed in a brochure. Such logic exemplifies the pragmatic yet visionary thinking often attributed to the self-effacing, 56-year-old information-age entrepreneur. Shih has been among the first to see the huge market for personal-computer clones, to focus on the big emerging markets of Latin America and Southeast Asia, and to adopt the build-to-order technique that now dominates the industry.

Since Acer's inception in 1976, its PCs have become best-sellers in 13 countries, including Mexico and the Philippines. In 1998, Acer was the fifth largest brand for mobile computers and the seventh largest brand for personal computers worldwide. Worldwide, the US$6.7-billion (1998 revenues) company produced an estimated one out of seven PCs in 1997. In 1999, the company's net income was US$382 million, up by 393.5% from the previous year's figures.

Volumes have been written about the man who put Taiwan on the computing map and his groundbreaking management style. A firm believer in decentralized management, Shih designed his organization to be a kind of "CEO factory." It has been reported that in 1990 he announced he would create 100 general managers by 1997—employees who run businesses, own Acer stock, take risks, and act like owners. He met his goal.

Shih has also created what he calls a "global federation of companies." Acer is broken into five highly autonomous business units that are publicly traded. He plans to give more investors a chance to buy a piece of Acer by launching 21 other such public companies by the twenty-first century. The idea is to make the company more nimble by giving its parts more autonomy.

Shih attributes his company's success to the "Acer Way," a philosophy which includes a corporate culture that emphasizes "human nature is basically good," the "fast-food business model," the "client-server" organizational structure, and the "global brand, local touch" strategy. In this article, he explains Acer's three major strategies and how they have contributed to the company's growth.

Acer's three major strategies all go against the traditional, control-oriented management model. The "fast-food business model" reverses the traditional vertical integration strategy. The "client-server" organizational structure destroys the hier-archical organization to adopt a decentralized operation. The "global brand, local touch" strategy shakes off the authoritative multinational management style to implement a worldwide partnership.

However, they are the prescriptions that have enabled Acer to survive difficulties and grow. To regain our competitiveness in speed and cost, we used the "fast-food business model" and moved computer assembly to the local marketplace. To solve the problem of management capability in the overseas assembly sites, we applied the "global brand, local touch" strategy and relied on local talent, even inviting them to become shareholders. To create an operational order for the decentralized operating sites all over the world, Acer established the "client-server" structure to consolidate the various organizations.

## The Fast-Food Business Model

I first used the fast-food concept to illustrate Acer's strategy during the company's worldwide distributors' meeting held in Mexico in 1992. I used the Chinese restaurant business as a metaphor to mirror the computer market.

Chinese restaurants are all over the world. Most customers find Chinese food delicious and inexpensive. However, these restaurants have a poor image because they are not run systematically and they suffer from inconsistent product quality.

Computer clone makers all over the world face a similar situation: They have poor product quality and an inferior image. On the other hand, McDonald's has become a worldwide fast-food chain store by having a simple menu, systematic operations, and one unified brand name. Hence, by adopting McDonald's operation model, we built on the strength of motherboard manufacturing while preventing its shortcomings.

As a result, Taiwan is Acer's "central kitchen" churning out components, including motherboards, housings, and monitors. The components are then air-shipped to regional business units overseas for local assembly.[1] In effect, each regional business unit becomes a fast-food store that assembles "fresh" PCs for local customers.

After adopting this model, Acer's inventory turnover rate improved 100%. The decline in inventory not only reduced operating risks for the company but also created the best condition for just-in-time introduction of new products.

After our business model was modified, Acer's products became more market-oriented. When Acer did the assembly in Taiwan, hot products were always short in supply and excess products were stocked in the warehouse. In 1998, Acer had 17 manufacturing sites and 30 assembly plants in 24 countries. As a result, we are able to flexibly build our products to local tastes and quickly respond to market changes.

## A Client-Server Organization

The client-server network is designed to connect various PCs in the office with the servers performing different functions so that a complete and

---

[1] As part of the fast-food model, Acer's components are classified in terms of how "perishable" they are. As reported in *A Fresh Perspective: The Acer Group Profile*, perishability is determined by how much risk is posed if they are held in inventory, or how sensitive components are to changing technology or fluctuations in market price. A component's perishability determines how it is shipped. Non-perishable components, like power supplies, are shipped via sea transport to keep costs low. The more perishable components, such as motherboards, are shipped via air transport to ensure fast delivery. The most perishable components, such as CPUs, are sourced locally.

flexible network is established.[2] The clients and servers are closely but flexibly connected to one another with every PC acting as an independently operated "client," and the "server" on the network ready to provide the best resource. The client-server network enjoys low cost, high efficiency, and great flexibility.

The same logic applies to Acer's organizational structure. Acer's business worldwide takes a local partnership approach. The center of decision-making is the shareholders' meeting in each business unit. The headquarters can only exercise its influence on business decisions through the shareholders' meeting.

In this management structure, each business unit plays the independent operating "client" as well as the support-providing "server" for other businesses. For example, Acer Peripherals Inc. is the "client" manufacturing monitors, while it is also the most professional and efficient "server" with economies of scale to provide products to the regional business units, which are responsible for regional and local sales and marketing operations.

In a centralized structure, all resources are concentrated in the headquarters. As a result, the headquarters takes all the risks. In a client-server structure, on the other hand, each unit is allowed to shoulder its own risks and make its own decisions.

The "client-server" structure facilitated the creation of the multimedia Aspire PC in 1995. Aspire is an important milestone in Acer's product development history, not because it reached annual sales of two million units in two years and achieved revenues of US$3 billion, but because it represents the success of Acer's client-server management system.

---

[2] In the client-server relationship of computer networks, the server is a central information storage PC that distributes information upon request, and the client is any PC requesting information. Applying this analogy to Acer's organizational structure, strategic business units (SBUs)—centralized manufacturing and product-development facilities that sell components—generally function as the servers. Regional business units (RBUs)—sales, marketing, and computer-assembly stations—act as the clients.

For the most part, the RBUs buy components from the SBUs (hence the client- server relationship), although SBUs also sell components to external clients and RBUs purchase components from external sources. But Acer's system also permits RBUs to become servers by developing their own products, which they distribute to both SBUs for component manufacture and to other RBUs for marketing in other regions.

I did not know much about the project when Acer America initiated it. Three months later, when I saw the charcoal-green computer box with its unique shape, I sensed that it would be a big hit in the computer industry. Within a short period of nine months, the Aspire was launched in the U.S. market and was a huge success.

Coordinated by Acer America, the Aspire was the result of the group's collective efforts. Acer America was in charge of the product concept, software interface, installation procedure, market planning, and promotion. Acer Peripherals Inc. and Acer Inc. were tasked with mechanical and electronic designs.

Television commercials were jointly produced in Singapore and New Zealand. Communications did not go through headquarters but were conducted directly among these different business units.

I believe that if Aspire went through our previous product development process—where reports were filed at headquarters and at many business units—it would have taken at least one and a half years to see the final product in the market. By that time, the daring creativity of the product might already have diminished.

## Global Brand, Local Touch

In the early 1990s, Acer's investments in overseas businesses suffered a huge loss. Suddenly, our shareholders and employees questioned our overseas investment plans. Some colleagues even openly challenged me and asked why the money they worked so hard to earn was lost in overseas operations.

As pressure mounted, I had to come up with solutions. It occurred to me that under the circumstances, the only way to convince our employees and investors was to invite our foreign partners to also invest in Acer and share the risk.

I first mentioned the strategy of "global brand, local touch" at the same distributors' meeting in Mexico in 1992. In my opening speech, I told Acer's partners from all over the world that "Acer is not only a Taiwan company. In the future, we will become a Mexican company." Later, we developed a complete version of the "global brand, local touch" strategy, which includes local shareholders, and the "21 in 21" concept, i.e., 21 publicly listed companies by the twenty-first century.

In March 1995, I visited Mexico again. By that time, Acer had already established a partnership of "local shareholder majority" with its Mexican partner. And a year before, Harvard University rated Acer the "most outstanding case study in globalization management."

The "21 in 21" strategy conveys an important message to all our colleagues around the world: "The company will be yours someday." Due to this strategy, Acer has created a basic environment for establishing solid partnerships and encouraged colleagues to reduce risks and quickly grasp opportunities.

## A Three-in-One System

The "fast-food business model," "client-server" structure, and local shareholders majority are a three-in-one mechanism. For instance, if there were no "client-server" structure when implementing the "fast-food business model," whenever a regional business unit ran into any difficulties with component supplies, it would rely on headquarters to solve the problem. But under the strategy of a "client-server" structure, each local operation is already a "client" with independent operating capability. It can no longer rely on headquarters for everything and will be forced to establish its own independent operation.

However, if there is no incentive for an overseas subsidiary to take operating responsibilities, it will still rely on headquarters eventually. Allowing the implementation of "local shareholders majority" will enable local executives to truly dedicate themselves to managing the company. Otherwise, the result of delegation only brings about failure to each unit.

Three reasons make me believe that "21 in 21" and a "client-server" structure will create an even more promising future for Acer:

First, under the structure, each business unit will take over its current operating responsibility. This gives me more time to consider Acer's future visions.

Secondly, since we operate in such a delegated environment, the vision which I develop will have to get everyone's consent. With consensus established, we have a greater chance of turning these visions into reality together.

Thirdly, if we do not share a common interest, any visionary strategy I come up with will have no strength to motivate the full cooperation of our colleagues. When Acer successfully builds up the basis of sharing common interests among its global partners, the momentum in implementing the strategies will become stronger and more powerful. ■

---

Excerpted from **"Me-Too Is Not My Style: Corporate Visions, Strategies, and Business Philosophies of the Acer Group"** by Stan Shih. © 1996 by the author. Reprinted by permission of the author. All rights reserved.

The biographical sketch was drawn using the following sources:

Condon, Bernard. "Dragon Under Pressure." *Forbes Global Business & Finance:* May 4, 1998.

Dumaine, Brian. "Asia's Wealth Creators Confront a New Reality." *Fortune:* December 8, 1997.

## Online Resources

- **Featured company**
  Acer Group
  http://www.acer.com.tw

- **Related articles**
  "Mach 3: Anatomy of Gillette's Latest Global Launch"
  By Glenn Rifkin
  Can a consumer product be launched globally in a short time? It can if sufficient resources and time are allocated to planning the effort.
  http://www.strategy-business.com/strategy/99205/

  "One with the Universe"
  By Sethuraman Dinakar
  Looking to reduce cycle times and improve customer service, companies in Asia are getting a whole lot smarter about managing their supply chains.
  http://www.cfoasia.com/archives/9907-40.htm

# The SGV Story:
# Values and the Human Factor

*Washington SyCip*

Founder, The SGV Group
Philippines

"Know your strengths as a business and develop them to the fullest: this has always been our guiding principle."

**Washington SyCip**

Washington SyCip has been called "the wise man of Manila." The 80-year-old founder of the regional accounting and management group SGV is known for his collection of owl images, all gifts from people who have benefited from his acumen.

SyCip received a fitting accolade in 1992 when he was given the Ramon Magsaysay Award for international understanding, a category of Asia's equivalent of the Nobel Prize. In naming him as one of its five awardees for that year, the Ramon Magsaysay Foundation observed that "Asia's rising tide of prosperity depends on its ability to compete." Recognizing this truism decades ago, "SyCip led his consulting company to preeminence by keeping it abreast of international standards and helping others in Asia to do the same."

In bringing modern accounting to the region, SyCip played a key role in propagating a common language of business and finance. SGV—originally SyCip, Gorres and Velayo—shared its expertise with accounting firms and leading enterprises in several Asian countries. More importantly, its number-crunchers showed other Asians that world-class accounting was not a preserve of the West.

SyCip says SGV lives by four guiding principles. One: "Whatever we do must be beneficial to the long-term interest of the country." Two: "Develop the full potential of every individual in our organization." Three: "Render the best service possible." And four: "Be absolutely fair in all our dealings."

In this article, he describes SGV's early challenges and the guiding principles that have helped it become one of the Philippines' best-regarded multinationals and Asia's leading management and auditing firm.

I n 1946, the Philippines was going through the painful process of recovering from the destruction wrought by World War II. Like many young men at that time, I wanted to be part of this effort. What we had then was the chance to reshape our destiny.

For all of us would-be entrepreneurs, this was a heady prospect. There were opportunities for growth in every conceivable area of business. In public accounting, these opportunities were tremendous, as the country needed accounting firms to work in partnership with the businesses that were then being revived.

Before the outbreak of the war, the Europeans managed the major professional firms in the countries now constituting ASEAN (Association of Southeast Asian Nations). Even exceptionally talented Asians, with many years of professional experience, would usually find themselves as subordinates to young Europeans or Americans with little knowledge of the country or its business practices.

Knowing full well the odds against me, I opened a one-man accounting office in one of the few buildings that had remained intact in Manila's Chinatown. I had an unusual experience of being the senior partner, the junior accountant, the messenger, and the janitor at the same time!

Later, I invited a long-time friend to join me. We worked tirelessly. To make ends meet, and out of a shared commitment to develop the Philippine accounting profession, we taught six nights a week at a Manila university.

Know your strengths as a business and develop them to the fullest: this had always been our guiding principle. As entrepreneurs with rather lofty ambitions, we were challenged by the difficulties we faced. We had to convince prospective clients of the value of an audit, particularly by such a new firm. And our competition included well-established foreign firms with extensive contacts among large corporations, which were mostly subsidiaries of foreign companies. Nevertheless, we kept our minds and bodies in peak condition to serve as many clients as we could.

However, competition was not our only problem. We wanted people who would create for the firm a reputation of dedicated service, efficiency, and professional integrity. Yet we were not in a position to offer young business graduates the salaries being paid by better-established firms.

It was probably fortunate for us that the foreign firms favored foreigners—and most of the local firms favored their owners' relatives. In short, there was no incentive for the bright university graduates to stay with foreign or local firms. We therefore focused much of our attention on recruiting the best talents in the field and offering training and growth opportunities within the firm. We assured the young men and women that they were limited only by their abilities, not by race or blood!

## Growth and Specialization

Not too long after we began, we became confident enough to put up branches in the major cities. Aided as we were by two mergers with smaller firms, we had grown quickly and were eager to expand our market. Primarily through training and research, we had kept up-to-date on developments in the profession.

We gradually became convinced that the lessons we were learning in building up a professional practice in our own country could be shared with other Asian professionals. This conviction led to our expansion beyond the Philippines. We recognized the benefits to be gained from involvement in the expanding market that was Asia.

The advantages of audit and management services, training programs, and research and computer facilities on a regional scale were obvious, and the thought of Asians helping other Asians in a region that was forging close economic ties was very attractive. With these objectives in mind, and with the support of a dedicated professional staff, we began to team up with other accountants throughout Asia to become the SGV Group.

In all these years of learning and sharing, we never lost sight of the need to improve our capabilities. In the early days, everyone, from partner down to junior, worked seven days a week, 10 to 12 hours a day, sometimes for months on end. Everyone had to be a jack-of-all-trades. For this reason, SGV was soon considered an excellent training ground for a beginning accountant. As the firm grew, however, specialization became possible and resulted in greater efficiency.

As our numbers and geographical reach increased, we also began to augment our audit, tax, and management services by organizing special groups within our ranks to address the specific needs of growing, as well as established, businesses and to service the country's and the region's growth requirements. For example, we set up a project development services division to provide the full range of services that an investor in a country would need—from the identification of a project to its startup.

We strengthened our capability in computers in anticipation of the importance of this technology to audit and consultancy work. To tap the market for computer training, we established the Institute of Advanced Computer Technology (I/ACT), a joint venture with Control Data Corporation of the United States. And to assist in the development of Asia's management resources, we established the SGV Development Center.

**Participating in the Nation's Progress**

These are just some of the activities we have undertaken in response to the changing needs of our clients. We were working along standard lines. We knew our strengths as a business and never set limits to what we could do; we knew our market and expanded it whenever we could; and we, like all good accountants, knew our financials.

From that first decision to participate in the national effort to regain what had been lost during the war, we maintained that the continued growth of a professional service firm is directly related to the prosperity of the country in which it operates. Thus we aligned our goals with those of the country, committing ourselves to the achievement of these goals.

When the nation built infrastructure, we serviced construction firms and utilities and transportation companies. When it sought to alleviate the problems of rapid urbanization, we helped with housing projects and marketing and distribution networks. When it placed top priority on achieving food self-sufficiency, we helped the producers, as well as the credit and irrigation institutions. To promote small-scale industry, we assisted the entrepreneurs. With feasibility studies and arrangements for joint ventures and financing packages, we eased the entry of foreign investment.

And underlying these services is what I consider our most significant contribution to the nation's development—the systematic training of the people who enter our doors. In all our 50-odd years, we had provided opportunities for professional advancement to all our staff, many of whom we had seen leaving us and becoming leaders in their fields.

Another of our values is the commitment to professionalism. Within the firm, this is seen in the unstinting willingness of staff members to place the interests of those they serve above their own personal interests, to find better ways to do their work and try new approaches, and to constantly strive to maintain high standards.

To maintain our professionalism, we have tried to be completely fair in our dealings with our clients and with everyone in our organization. With regard to our own people, we have always given maximum incentives to those who are competent and able to move ahead, disregarding the seniority system. Promotions have been based on merit and, unlike many Asian organizations, nepotism has never been practiced.

An aspect of our commitment to professionalism is our insistence on high standards of work. We do not simply acquire clients and service their professed needs. We get to know our clients intimately—their products, methods of production, distribution channels, financial policies, and positions in the industry. We help create for them the right environment in which to grow.

From the very beginning, we realized that our ability as a firm to offer the best type of service hinges on the competence of our people. To use accounting terms, we continuously try to increase staff members' assets and decrease their liabilities so that their net worth to the firm and to our clients increases from year to year. We have pursued this commitment through structured and practical training at all levels, even sending our staff to the leading graduate schools in the United States and Europe.

In all the countries in which we have taken root, we place great value on the use of local human resources. Because we are a professional organization operating in a developing country environment, we need people who possess a fundamental understanding of the culture and conditions in developing countries.

This reliance on national resources has given us an advantage. As a multinational, we have the breadth of experience which we share with all the member firms, thus enabling us to adapt the approaches of more developed economies to meet the needs of developing countries not only in Asia but also in other parts of the world. Being in a number of countries at different stages of their economic development also gives our people the ability to see what is forthcoming. Through the lessons learned in one country, we can help our clients in another country anticipate developments and take necessary steps.

We believe that change is both inevitable and necessary. We therefore plan for it. We have never hesitated to modify our management attitudes to make our firm attractive to bright young people. Our system of recognition ensures that the leadership of our firm remains in the hands of people who are willing and able to learn and apply new knowledge.

We welcome innovation in the ways we offer our services and develop, use, and conserve our resources. We have always been afraid of becoming complacent. This is why we experiment. For example, we have adopted the total service concept, which assures greater receptivity to our clients' needs.

These principles and values have brought us to where we are now in the economic and professional fields. But beyond these achievements, we know our responsibility to the public. In all the countries in which we are represented, we have been actively supporting professional organizations and have set up foundations dedicated to the promotion of the social and economic welfare of the country.

In the Philippines, SGV was a founding member of the Philippine Business for Social Progress, an organization funded by private businesses to undertake socio-economic development projects. We also established the SGV Professional/Social Investment Program, under which we donate our services to organizations that aim to ameliorate the conditions of disadvantaged groups.

There have been some disappointments through these years and cases of professionals who were interested only in maximizing their incomes and who often forgot moral values. But, as in all human endeavors, one must expect a certain number of failures. My only advice to all entrepreneurs is to quickly throw out the rotten banana before it contaminates the good fruit.

Whether in business or the professions, one quickly learns that high ethical standards and a willingness to learn and change must back leadership qualities. Do we have too lofty principles for a professional firm? Perhaps. But these principles and our adherence to them over the years have come to characterize the SGV Group. And as I think of the many clients whom we have assisted in their efforts to make the countries of this region a better place to live in, I can only say that we are fortunate to have been given the opportunity to participate in the exciting process of development. ■

---

Excerpted from "**Asian Perspectives on Business and Management, Economic Success, and Governance: East Asia, Oceania, the Philippines, and SGV**" by Washington SyCip. © 1996 by SGV & Co. Published by the University of the Philippines Press. All rights reserved.

The biographical sketch was drawn using the following source:
Lopez, Antonio. "The Gospel of SGV." *Asiaweek:* September 18, 1992.

## Online Resources

- **Related articles**

"Aligning Action and Values"
By Jim Collins
Executives spend too much time crafting vision statements, mission statements, values statements, and so on. They spend nowhere near enough time trying to align their organizations with the values and visions already in place.
http://www.pfdf.org/leaderbooks/l21/summer96/collins.html

"Hire Today, Gone Tomorrow?"
By Scott Kirsner
Tough question: How can you hold onto your best people? Honest answer: You probably can't. The real goal is to keep great people working with you, even after they've stopped working for you.
http://www.fastcompany.com/online/16/hiretoday.html

"The Training Myth"
By Jack Stack
The most valuable employee training usually comes from on-the-job experience, not from a formal training session. This article offers ways to empower employees to learn for themselves.
http://www.inc.com/incmagazine/archives/08980411.html

# Teams on Fire:
# Sony's Innovation Culture

*Nobuyuki Idei*

*Chairman and Chief Executive Officer, Sony Corporation*
*Japan*

"We take risks for innovations we believe in, and we put our faith not only in that great impersonal called *technology* but in gifted individuals who have unique capacities to imagine, and to engineer and manufacture what they imagine."

**Nobuyuki Idei**

All eyes are on Sony's PlayStation 2 (PS2), its most advanced home video game system yet. To be sure, the electronics firm's original PlayStation is already a cash cow for Sony. In the fiscal year ended March 1999, operating profit from the game and software accounted for 40% of the firm's US$2.8 billion operating profit.

But Sony has a lot more than short-term profits riding on the PS2. If all goes according to CEO Nobuyuki Idei's plan, the top-of-the-line game console—with its DVD player for viewing full-length films, multiple ports for easy access to the Net or add-ons such as a computer hard-disk drive, and powerful microprocessor, which can be hooked up to a VCR, cable TV, a keyboard, mouse, or printer—will do more than just play games. The PS2 could emerge as the hub of the home network, downloading content while serving as a gateway to the Web.

With its long tradition of innovative products and savvy marketing, Sony has done more than any other company to define consumer electronics. Now, as the 63-year-old Idei sees it, the company needs to bridge the gap between its core businesses of electronics—TVs, stereos, and the like—and its rich pool of content, such as music, movies, video games, and financial services that run on the electronics.

The outspoken chief executive is determined to transform the world's leading maker of consumer electronics into an agile player on the Web. And it won't be an easy task. For one, Idei realizes that the old management style no longer works at Sony. "We don't have time to build a consensus," he says. "We need swimmers. I have been throwing onlookers into the water."

Also, it hardly helps that in one market after another—films, PCs, mobile communications—Sony is looking lackluster. Even Sony Computer Entertainment Inc., which manufactures PS2, faces formidable competition from Microsoft Corp., which plans to invade the game market with a souped-up console.

Against this background, Idei still believes that the company's "innovation culture" will be key in transforming Sony into an Internet company. In this article, he describes the company's "twin heritage in innovation and marketing."

On May 11, 1999, Sony launched a new industry. The occasion was a product launch in central Tokyo, to which video and print journalists had been invited from Japanese and international media. All eyes and cameras were focused on our first market-ready digital creature—a long-eared, frisky, four-legged entertainment robot named AIBO.

AIBO bats a ball, wags his tail, barks, and nods his head quizzically, among other things. And he proved to be an instant hit with consumers: The 3,000 units available in Japan from our first manufacturing run, offered exclusively at the Sony Web site, sold out in 20 minutes. AIBO appeared in the *Wall Street Journal*, *Business Week*, and many other publications worldwide.

As we introduced AIBO to journalists, we emphasized a number of business points. We made clear our belief that robotics will be an important twenty-first century industry and our desire at Sony to provide creative, technological, and commercial leadership in the field. We also stated our conviction that no one company should dominate; the industry will move forward vigorously only when several companies bring intellectual and financial resources to it.

The journalists were naturally curious to know what comes next. In response to that inquiry, Dr. Toshitada Doi, the director of Sony's Digital Creatures Laboratory, provided two answers. First, the name of our lab implies that we plan to develop a digital menagerie of entertainment robots that will be increasingly mobile and fun, and will be endowed with intriguing character design as the technology evolves. Second, Doi explained that the technologies developed for entertainment robots could be applied to devices that do serious work, such as rescue and mine clearing. By developing small-scale entertainment robots today, we are laying the foundation of an industry that will serve some of society's critical needs.

I start with this tale of an entertainment robot because I want to convey at once that Sony innovates. We take risks for innovations we believe in, and we put our faith not only in that great impersonal called technology but in gifted individuals who have unique capacities to imagine, and to engineer and manufacture what they imagine. We don't place our trust in market surveys or today's business successes. Our goal is to create new markets by discovering hidden, perhaps even unrecognized, needs and wishes. We do not imitate. This is the proudest and most challenging value in our culture.

## Designing Products for the Digital Network Era

All Sony employees respect the company's twin heritage in innovation and marketing, which goes back to the two founders. The late Masaru Ibuka was the technology genius, the product innovator. His inquisitive mind and ability to make the difficult seem easy have passed into our culture. The late Akio Morita was the marketing genius, the one who traveled abroad soon after the end of the second world war to get Sony into the minds and hearts of customers outside of Japan.

What we inherit from these two individuals are their values and energy and the unified Sony brand. Today's world differs very much from theirs. To my mind, the watershed events separating the first 50 years from the next 50 are the convergence of previously separate technologies and the rise of the Internet.

At Sony we think a lot about the emerging digital network era. This concept has two meanings for us, one internal, the other external. Internally it means that all of us within Sony are engaged in modifying our business models, R&D, and product designs to take into account that products for today's world must be networked, that is, connected and used together. We expect a PC-centric or an advanced audio-video device to serve as a platform for connectivity and interoperability. Externally, our emphasis on the emerging networked society communicates to the outside world that this is the trend and that Sony is there. We will continue to be a leading player as more and more products gain network capabilities.

Sony focuses on consumer electronics for the home, and we are interested in the home network—a new configuration of devices and functions with the TV as a hub, which has not yet assumed definite shape. The powerful and novel chips at the heart of our PlayStation—the Emotion Engine and the Graphics Synthesizer—suggest to many of us applications in the home that go well beyond games. Today, those chips make possible a delightfully realistic new experience of movie-like action, generated in real time as directed by the game player. Tomorrow, we shall discover what the wider capabilities of the chips may be.

Some consumers are already experiencing and exploring the emerging home network. For example, users of our VAIO C1 PictureBook computer can record a digital photograph or video clip on its built-in camera, edit that content on a screen, insert it into an organizational newsletter, a home page, or a personal e-mail, and dispatch it worldwide. The computer is a camera and video recorder; the camera and video recorder are a computer—this is convergence. There is more than a trend here: There is inevitability.

### Organizational Innovation: Managing Complexity

Our co-founder, Akio Morita, didn't hesitate to reorganize the company as our businesses diversified and grew, and as markets changed. We have again followed his example through a far-reaching reorganization intended to make Sony as optimally creative, efficient, and profitable participant in the new markets of the digital network era as possible.

Our goal is to encourage the independence of our businesses while ensuring that each business helps the others. We have learned that while each independent business influences the others and shares content or technology with them, a new event can occur for which I have borrowed from science the term "emergent evolution". Emergent evolution means that important innovations can emerge from the interaction of parts within the complex whole of Sony.

My personal challenge is to create that new business model, a platform for emergent evolution across Sony. In March 1999, we announced our new "integrated decentralized" model. Through this new configuration, I am convinced that our businesses can best serve the networked society of the coming century and generate still greater value for our shareholders.

Our electronics businesses are being redefined as network companies, and each is empowered to operate with considerable independence and to develop its own portfolio of venture investments. Sony corporate headquarters has already begun to transfer to the companies essential support functions and R&D laboratories. A somewhat smaller headquarters will provide coordination while operating its own venture portfolio and retaining direct responsibility for certain businesses charged with developing strategies and technologies for the network business model.

Comparable changes are being instituted in our entertainment and other businesses, all to one purpose: to create vigorous enterprises that interact in strikingly creative ways, under the overall direction of a smaller corporate headquarters. Not least among our organizational innovations is our effort to revise our board of directors and create a new level of corporate executive officers, to distinguish more clearly between those individuals responsible for oversight and those responsible for management. Sony could emerge in the future as a holding company with a portfolio of extremely vital, productive businesses and a more incisive and empowered board. Whatever path we take, it will always be toward managing complex businesses with great effectiveness, relating them effectively to one another, and freeing them to achieve more than ever before.

**Toward Team Creativity and Passion**

Dr. Toshitada Doi and I have been colleagues for many years, and in our conversations we sometimes touch on what allows R&D teams to catch fire and become capable of a high level of achievement. Aside from being the director of our Digital Creatures Laboratory, he was a principal developer of the compact disc. I suppose he understands as much as anybody about teams on fire with creativity and directed passion.

The surprising thing in a man who has achieved so much of a practical nature is that Doi doesn't approach the subject strictly from a project management perspective. The inner qualities of team members and their relationships and the capacity for vision and objectivity in the leader matter more to him than anything else.

"The team must have a certain purity," he once told me. "It must be free from political distortions—from animosity between team members, from egoistic ambition, and from internal pressure to make technical compromises. It must also be free from top management distortion by which I take him to be warning me to approve worthwhile projects, fund them, and then step courteously away while the real work gets done.

"When this is so," Doi continued, "all participants can concentrate on the technology, and the team as a whole may catch fire—truly 'switch on' and enter a different state. It's not very logical, but when that switch occurs, everything is possible. We'll face difficulties, but the difficulties will go away. Under these conditions the team *calls its destiny*. Its fate is different than it would have been."

I once took the position with Doi that the leader must be close to the team, must mix in and share every burden.

"No," he replied, "the leader must have a certain distance."

I asked him what he meant. "Think of a vehicle moving through unknown territory," he said, "and imagine a bird up above it, looking ahead, seeing what comes next. That's the leader's distance."

It seems to end here, with two fellows in conversation about the sources of profound and truly useful innovation. ■

---

Excerpted from **"Wisdom of the CEO: 29 Global Leaders Tackle Todays Most Pressing Business Challenges"** by G. William Dauphinais, Grady Means, and Colin Price. Copyright 2000 by PricewaterhouseCoopers LLP. Published by John Wiley & Sons, Inc. All rights reserved.

The biographical sketch was drawn using the following sources:

Dawson, Chester. "Sony Plays to Win." *Far Eastern Economic Review*: March 2, 2000.

Kunii, Irene. "The Slump at Sony." *Business Week*: June 5, 2000.

Murakami, Mutsuko. "Reinventing a Giant." *Asiaweek*: January 28, 2000.

## Online Resources

- **Featured company**
  Sony Corporation
  http://www.world.sony.com

- **Related articles**
  "A Matter of Style"
  By Chester Dawson
  For legions of loyal consumers worldwide, Sony is synonymous with style. Reason enough for the Japanese electronics maker to work diligently to maintain its hard-won reputation.
  http://www.feer.com/_0005_25/p65innov.html

  "Innovation: Survival of the Fittest"
  By Charles Leadbeater
  The best way for large organizations to work through the dilemmas posed by innovation is to borrow from the most powerful innovative force in the world: biological evolution.
  http://www.ac.com/ideas/Outlook/1.2000/over_innovation.html

# Treating "Big-Business Syndrome"

## Kazuma Tateisi

*Founder and Former Chairman, Omron Corporation*
*Japan*

"Big-business syndrome is characterized by a highly centralized and swollen bureaucracy; a proliferation of special forms to handle routine decisions; increasing numbers of meetings to reach decisions; and transference of problems between departments."

**Kazuma Tateisi**

Organizational well-being, like physical health, depends on discovering what causes symptoms of imbalance in the system. Troubled by the erosion in his company's ability to respond to customer demands, Kazuma Tateisi, the late founder of Omron Corp., analyzed the signals of "big-business syndrome" and suggested ways to enable technological innovation and the entrepreneurial spirit to flourish as companies grow in his book, *The Eternal Venture Spirit*.

In his preface to the Japanese edition of the book, Kenichi Ohmae marvels that even though Tateisi described incidents that took place when he was a middle-aged executive, he still possessed the resolve to build a multibillion-dollar company and seek new challenges at every turn. Ohmae notes that, like a scientist, Tateisi had an innate curiosity and was ahead of his time. He writes, "In pursuing the abstract fields of automation, he had no models. Practically all of the early projects were sketched out on the basis of an idea and an image of the future." For example, the credit card vending machines that Omron developed found no market at the time.

Tateisi would have been proud of the company he founded in 1933. Omron has stayed faithful to his vision and is now a leader in the field of automation with over 23,000 employees in over 35 countries around the world and sales of US$4.6 billion in 1999. The company makes automation components and systems—ranging from automated teller machines to digital blood pressure monitors—which use fuzzy logic, open platform, sensing, and life science technologies.

In the following article, Tateisi discusses how companies can avoid the pitfalls of stagnation from a "central nervous system" that has grown too large to communicate with itself.

I n mid-1983, we at Omron Tateisi Electronics carried out a corporate reorganization to eradicate a disease that had wormed its way into Omron—a sickness I call "big-business syndrome." Big-business syndrome can be recognized by the following symptoms: a highly centralized and swollen bureaucracy; a proliferation of special forms to handle routine decisions; increasing numbers of meetings to reach decisions; and transference of problems between departments.

Final decisions are put off because executives are unwilling to accept specific responsibility. As a result, instructions to the front line, the actual site of the problem, are delayed indefinitely until oversight turns into authority. Such erosion of an organization's ability to respond destroys any mindset of efficiency that may have existed before.

## The Symptoms

I first noticed these symptoms at Omron in the fall of 1981. I noticed that internal response had slowed appreciably. When inventory was swollen, for example, even specific orders to "reduce inventory" could not cause it to subside readily. I noticed, too, that response to external demands was much slower. Our ability to respond quickly to customers' requests had eroded.

When we were smaller and a customer asked us to modify or create a product, the sales representative would quickly report the demand, whereupon the technicians would make the parts without any drawings. If the assembled prototype looked satisfactory, it would be taken straight to the customer. The preliminaries would then be settled and we'd have the order on the spot. The whole process would take less than two weeks.

By the early 1980s, however, two or three months were required for such a transaction. Customers' requests require timely response. If we do not meet their needs quickly, they'll go to someone who can.

In the control equipment business, the mainstay of Omron's operations, the 40% market share that we had relied on through the late 1970s had fallen in less than five years to 37%. The key reason for this decline was a steady loss of customers precipitated by a slow response to their demands. This was clearly a symptom of big-business syndrome.

"People don't usually like to talk about trouble, but since things have come this far, I think you should all be aware of what's going on." These were my words to a group of union leaders at an informal labor-management meeting in early 1983.

I expressed my view that big-business syndrome was eating into the company. I explained how our lagging response to user needs has driven away even some of our steady customers and how our corporate structure is so swollen that it cannot feel the pain.

That said, we adjourned to a small restaurant in Kyoto, where the executives and the union officials exchanged views while plucking food from a hotpot. The opinion of the young union leaders came as a surprise.

"Mr. Tateisi, we were very glad to hear what you said today," they told me.

"How can you be happy to hear such bad news?" I asked.

They replied, "Well, even if we were apprehensive before, it couldn't have helped. But today, none other than the chairman of the board himself sounded the alarm—and offered a prescription for curing the problem. Now we know that the people at the top are sincerely worried, and that's why we are happy."

When I heard that, I was happy, too. If we played our cards right, we could surely revitalize Omron.

## The Cure

A few days later, at a nationwide organization of our sales agents, I gave the insiders the same speech that I had given to the union leaders. Immediately afterward, I was surrounded by seven or eight sales representatives who were just as delighted as those young union reps had been.

During the conversation, I asked the sales agents about Thanks, a photoelectric-switch venture business in Nagoya with about 300 employees, which was taking business away from them. I was overwhelmed to find out how Thanks had grabbed market share by moving boldly into the gaps in the Omron product line.

But that wasn't all, I now learned. On countless orders, even when customers were looking for difficult labor-saving improvements, the venture firm had dealt with the problems, won the customers' hearts, and gobbled up more of our business.

The robust vitality of Thanks was exactly the same sort of strength that Omron had thrived on 30 years earlier. I understood then that to cure big-business syndrome, it was necessary for Omron to operate once again as if it were a small business.

**Treatment**

So we implemented a corporate restructuring in June 1983. At that time, we had about 5,300 employees. To infuse in everyone's consciousness the spirit behind this restructuring, we chose three slogans for everyone to repeat daily: "everyone sells," "quick response," and "quick action." Each morning, employees were to recite these slogans instead of the usual greetings, so that the ideas behind them would be fixed in their minds as they went about their business.

There were two pillars of the restructuring plan. One was to bring top management closer to actual working conditions. The other was to create several small divisions that would be given complete autonomy and would operate as small businesses within the company.

To achieve the first pillar, we abolished the top decision-making body, the nine-member management committee of the board of directors. In its place, we created an executive committee consisting of the top three officers of the company—the chairman, the president, and the vice-president.

While the management committee had been meeting twice monthly, the streamlined executive committee—adopting as its motto "lightning attack"—met weekly. As a result, the decisions of the three executive members were made very quickly.

The other pillar of the reorganization, the small-division system, consisted of divisional headquarters based on our primary markets. Most

*Kazuma Tateisi*

of our key competitors were small-venture businesses. By thoroughly decentralizing authority into small-business divisions, we made each of our operations about the same scale as that of our rivals. We aimed to foster a change in consciousness by whipping up a mentality of rivalry.

On the basis of that thinking, we first created a divisional headquarters for each of our four main markets: control components, electronic fund transfer systems, public service systems, and office automation systems. Eventually, we created 20 divisions. These 20 strategic business units were commissioned to perform everything from R&D to overseas marketing.

When I looked back a little more than a year after implementing the new structure, I could see that clear progress had been made. For one thing, the amount of time required to fulfill a customer's specifications for some new item became precisely fixed. Employees identified which modifications would take several days and which prototype developments would take three months. Also, the traditional misguided notion that "exports are naturally slower" had been reformed.

Seeing these changed conditions, I pronounced that big-business syndrome had been 70% cured. Improvement was visible in the business results reported for fiscal year 1984, ending 31 March.

The year began under the old system. At the beginning of the term, an annual sales total of 187.1 billion yen was projected. However, since we effected the restructuring in June 1983, in November the figure was revised to 200.3 billion yen. At that point, I thought we had licked big-business syndrome and growth accelerated even more.

In January 1984, the estimate was again increased, to 205 billion yen. At year's end, the actual sales figure for fiscal year 1984 was 208.8 billion yen—27% higher than the previous year's performance. This was evidence of the revolution in consciousness that resulted from the restructuring. ■

---

From **"The Eternal Venture Spirit"** by Kazuma Tateisi. © 1989 by Productivity, Inc., (www.productivityinc.com), PO Box 13390, Portland, OR 97213-0390, tel: (800) 394 6868. Reprinted by permission.

87

# Online Resources

- **Featured company**
  Omron Corporation
  http://www.omron.com

- **Related articles**
  "Bureaucracy Busting"
  By Craig Cantoni
  Ten ways to break down bureaucracies
  http://www.smartbiz.com/sbs/arts/exe196.htm

  "Think Small, Win Big"
  By Bob Davis and Terri Austerberry
  How can companies get managers to act as owners of their businesses? How can they attract and retain talented people who are not afraid to take risks? And how can they develop and commercialize innovative ideas before their competitors? A new organizational model offers a possible answer.
  http://mckinseyquarterly.com/article_page.asp?articlenum=327

# Power to the People

## Kumar Mangalam Birla

*Chairman, The Aditya Birla Group*
*India*

"Cultivating a new generation of managers, employee empowerment and delegation, and fostering a participative culture are keys to the increasingly energetic, people-centered, and performance-focused culture that we aspire for."

**Kumar Mangalam Birla**

May 28, 1999 was a red-letter day for Kumar Mangalam Birla. On that day, the chairman of the Aditya Birla Group, India's second largest industrial house, with aggregate sales of US$2.8 billion, participated in a 360-degree feedback session. Forty-two senior managers, who directly reported to him, rated him on his leadership style, managerial ability, and even personal traits.

The verdict: the 34-year-old Birla empowered his managers, delegated well, and had a vision. However, he was not clearly articulating his expectations from his managers. As a result, two months after the exercise, each senior manager received a six-page personal letter from Birla, assessing his respective role, mentioning areas that required improvement, and spelling out his expectations.

Such a feedback session may be standard operating procedure at many leading-edge companies, but at the 89-year-old business group, it was truly a radical departure from convention. At the Aditya Birla Group, the CEO's word had traditionally been obeyed implicitly, no questions asked. Until Birla assumed the mantle of leadership in 1995.

Since then the fourth-generation manager has instituted earth-shaking changes. After scrapping the group's famous "womb to tomb" employment policy, he instituted a performance appraisal system across the group and a program for tracking and developing high-potential managers, which includes developing skills, inter-unit transfers, and overseas assignments. He has personally led recruitment campaigns into business schools and launched the Aditya Birla Scholarships to foster excellence among the student community and nurture the leaders of tomorrow.

Birla realizes that the only way he can continue to effectively manage a group with 35 companies in 14 countries and 140,000 employees in an intensively competitive environment is to foster a people-centered organization. In this

article, adapted from a 1998 article which the authoritative CEO wrote for
*Aditya*—the group's management journal—and various speeches, he elaborates
on the human resource strategies that are energizing his organization's culture.

W e operate today in an unforgiving, rapidly changing,
globally competitive business environment. Traditionally,
our fundamental strengths have been in the areas of
relentless productivity improvements, innovative cost cutting, and
operating efficiencies. These fundamental strengths have enabled us to
face the most turbulent times with fortitude.

But these strengths are not enough. To remain at the cutting edge, we
have to focus not only on our operational strategies but also, more
importantly, on our "people power," and foster a people-centered and
performance-focused culture. For it is our people alone who take our
group to glorious heights.

Realizing this, our group has been consciously veering toward
unleashing people power in a well-planned manner. We have put in
place groupwide human resources systems, which aim to cultivate a new
generation of managers, empower employees, and foster a participative culture.

## Making Room at the Top

If we are inducting people at the lower rungs, but the top echelons of the
organization are getting clogged and people aren't leaving in a systematic
manner, then the career paths of middle- and lower-level executives get
blocked. A new generation of managerial talent waits in the wings, eager
to prove their abilities in top positions and explore new opportunities.
It is our collective responsibility to see that their aspirations are fulfilled.

Our retirement policy, which fixes the retirement age at 60 for everyone
except the directors of the Birla Management Center, has two objectives:
to facilitate the smooth transition of senior employees into retirement and
to provide room at the top for the second line to grow. It also makes
succession planning simpler. For example, in September 2000, 120
managers will retire, creating senior-level vacancies. Because we know

exactly when vacancies will arise, it is only a question of evaluating who the successors will be.

## Creating an Army of Skilled Managers

Our recruitment process hinges on the belief that one of the most important jobs of top management is to ensure the development of people to lead tomorrow's organization. Given the primacy of people, we have set up a Group Management Trainee Scheme, which aims to create a common management cadre at the entry level. The objective of the program is nothing short of creating a management army for the future.

The trainees are selected from graduates of premier educational institutes and young professionals already working in our units. For young graduates, this program is a dream come true. For those already employed in the group, this will be a route for them to fast-track their career progress.

The trainees undergo a rigorous and comprehensive year-long program during which they will obtain an overview of the group, as well as exposure to a small unit, a medium-sized unit, and a large unit, to give them an appreciation of different challenges in varying management situations. In addition, they will be given the opportunity to work in an overseas unit and will be put in charge of a function in a small or medium-sized unit.

After their one-year training, the management trainees will remain a vital resource for the group. These young professionals bring relevant analytical skills and a fresh perspective so necessary in today's business scenario. We should take advantage of their enthusiasm and drive. As long as they remain top performers, we will continue to track their career development and ensure that they acquire critical managerial skills.

## Bottom-Driven, Not Top-Heavy

The need to nurture leaders for a large group like the Aditya Birla Group can never be emphasized enough. What I want is an approach that provides empowerment and delegation at all levels based on people competence. To make our organization bottom-driven rather than top-heavy is the responsibility of every unit head and those at the level below him.

For unit heads to find out how their colleagues and bosses rate them on the level of empowerment and delegation that they practice, I encourage them to enlist in the 360-degree feedback program organized by our group's HR department. Many unit heads have gone through this learning experiment and are using the revelations to bridge the gap between the perception, the reality, and the ideal. We should all benchmark ourselves against the best of the business leaders.

Bear in mind that the intensifying competition brought about by globalization requires employees at the front to be as determined to succeed as those in the rear. By pushing responsibility to frontline employees, giving them trust and recognition, we can harness and release the capabilities of all our people.

## Tapping Employees' Valuable Ideas

Coping with the challenges of a globally competitive scenario calls for tapping the unleashed ideas of our employees across the board. It also entails an increasingly participative culture. I believe that, in the times ahead, our only sustainable advantage will come from constantly reinventing our group and getting more and more out of our people who can think "out of the box" with implementable ideas that assure us of retaining the edge.

To concretize this idea, we launched "We Will Win (WWW)," a groupwide initiative which aims to garner increased participation from our pool of managerial talent. We started by involving 150 executives whose participation resulted in 30 suggestions for implementation. As the WWW theme gains momentum, I hope to include many more colleagues. We will use the collective wisdom generated by the WWW project to better our people-related, customer-oriented systems, and organizational process management.

Most of our HR policies are in response to our employees' desire for empowerment, leadership positions, continuous learning, and an atmosphere of mutual respect and transparency, which they articulated in an organizational health study conducted in 1997. In esssence, what we have been trying to do is incubate management talent and foster leadership processes internally to help us bravely face challenges that an externally turbulent environment poses. In this manner, we can nurture the next generation of stars to leave behind a legacy of talent which can carry our group forward toward good times as well as tough times. ■

The biographical sketch was drawn using the following sources:

Balse, Hemangi. "Kumar Birla's Brave New World." *Business Standard:* January 2, 1999.

Jayakar, Roshni. "Leading People the Kumar Birla Way." *Business Today:* October 7, 1999.

## Online Resources

- **Featured company**
  The Aditya Birla Group
  http://www.adityabirla.com/

- **Related articles**
  "How to Give Good Feedback"
  By Gina Imperato
  People won't get great at their jobs unless you do a great job of giving them feedback. So why are performance reviews the most hated ritual in business? Here's a five-point program to improve your performance with reviews.
  http://www.fastcompany.com/online/17/feedback.html

  "Writing the Book on Managing Employees"
  By Jeffrey L. Seglin
  Reviews of seven business books, including *The Three Keys To Empowerment: Release the Power Within People for Astonishing Results* and *First, Break All the Rules: What the World's Greatest Managers Do Differently.* Subjects include employee motivation, the seven deadly sins of business, and tips on running a family business.
  http://www.inc.com/incmagazine/archives/06991111.html

# Applying Business Rigor to a Humanitarian Mission

*Sadako Ogata*

*High Commissioner for Refugees*
*The Office of the United Nations*
*Switzerland*

"Our dependence on voluntary funding has kept us on our toes. If we disappoint our stakeholders, they can slash their contributions and drastically curtail the effectiveness of the services we provide for people in extremis."

**Sadako Ogata**

Sadako Ogata, 74, has been High Commissioner for Refugees since the late 1990s. Since then, this soft-spoken woman has shown an iron will and enormous drive in her campaign to improve her organization's delivery of a vast range of services to refugees, whose numbers have increased during her tenure from 19 million to 26 million.

Unlike other United Nations agencies, the office of the UN High Commissioner for Refugees (UNHCR) gets little regular funding from the UN budget. Most of its US$1.3-billion budget comes from voluntary contributions. This means that the UNHCR must establish and maintain a reputation for efficiency with a large population of donors and stakeholders.

The UNHCR presents a management challenge even more complex than most multinational corporations. It employs some 5,500 people, working out of 255 offices in 123 countries—typically under conditions of great instability and often physical danger. In turn, these staffers work in local partnership with over 450 non-government organizations (NGOs) to protect, feed, repatriate, and resettle refugees in situations where what can go wrong often does.

In this article, Ogata describes how she has applied business rigor to the UNHCR's humanitarian mission and developed a framework that outlines the skills, knowledge, and attributes which a staff member must have to be effective within the UNHCR—both at headquarters and in the field. The result: At a time when the United States has been accusing the UN and its agencies of managerial inefficiency, the UNHCR has been acknowledged as a sound operation.

One thing which private and non-private institutions share is that they both have stakeholders. To serve these stakeholders, they have to demonstrate responsiveness in delivering their mission and operational efficiency. The lucky institutions are those with stakeholders who are vigilant about ferreting out shortcomings.

In this sense, the UNHCR has been fortunate. Our dependence on voluntary funding has kept us on our toes, since the value of our work with refugees and the methods by which work is done are reappraised every year.

This is analogous to the scrutiny of a corporation by its public shareholders, only it is more exigent, since disappointed stakeholders can slash their contributions and thus drastically curtail the range and effectiveness of the services that the UNHCR provides for people in extremis. Under these circumstances, it is easy to forget that refugees are first and foremost individuals, not an abstract problem. The "problem" approach tends to lead to insensitivity, inadequate refugee relief, and ultimately to disenchanted stakeholders.

The UNHCR cannot afford to sacrifice a generation of refugees because it is trying to be efficient at a given time. It is our policy never to walk away from pressing human needs until the job is done.

I'd like to discuss two of the initiatives that have made the UNHCR's stakeholders increasingly aware of the plight of refugees, as well as convinced them that their contributions are being deployed with maximum efficiency. Both these initiatives are concerned with re-deploying headquarters' resources and policies in a way that strengthens the efforts, morale, and productivity of the staffers in the field who are in direct contact with the UNHCR's refugee "customers."

The barometer of stakeholder confidence has to be constantly monitored. In April 1991, three months after my appointment, the UNHCR faced a situation that could have seriously damaged donor confidence. Over a period of three weeks, 450,000 Kurds fled toward the Turkish border with the armies of Saddam Hussein on their heels. At the same time, another 1.25 million Kurds moved toward Iran. As the refugees fled to this harsh, desolate mountain border range in mid-winter, it quickly became clear that no agency was equipped to respond effectively to this enormous crisis.

Unfortunately, the UNHCR was hamstrung by the internationally accepted definition that a refugee has to have crossed an international border. Since the Kurds were still within the confines of Iraq, we could not mobilize resources as swiftly as the need demanded, nor did we have the resources to cope with 1.7 million refugees.

As a result, in 1991 the UNHCR created the Emergency Preparedness and Response Section (EPRS). This new unit has the ability to send fully trained operational teams to meet emergency conditions in the field within 72 hours. Every UNHCR section volunteers staff for the EPRS, which is run by a small core group. These volunteers are trained as a team and remain on 24-hour standby for six months.

Since its creation, the EPRS has been deployed in many parts of the world whose names read like a checklist of humanitarian crises. The EPRS had set up an airlift into beleaguered Sarajevo in 1992 and organized the relief effort for one of the largest refugee crises ever, the exodus of 1.2 million Rwandans into eastern Zaire in mid-1994.

By redefining global ideas of who a refugee is, and by creating what was, in effect, a relief SWAT team, the UNHCR has demonstrated its capacity to galvanize its forces with speed and effectiveness in response to emergency situations. These efforts have also helped focus attention on the underlying problem—the ongoing need to create a positive influence on world opinion to protect potential refugee populations.

A second field-empowering initiative gives relief workers in the field the tools they need to respond flexibly and swiftly on their own without all the checking back with headquarters that previous systems required. Changes are already being implemented across a two-year time frame. Project DELPHI, as the program is known, has been managed internally and has thus far involved most of the UNHCR staff. As a result, it has created a broad internal commitment to change.

However, for empowerment to work, the UNHCR must be sure that its field staff have the right attitudes and the competencies to use their authority properly. In the past, there have been communication problems between headquarters and the field. There were also problems of delegating authority and resources.

In response, there has been an effort over the past two years to implement a Career Management System that enables the UNHCR staff to align individual performance with overall agency strategy, as well as providing a clear framework for personal development. This scheme is built around six core competencies and six managerial competencies that outline the skills, knowledge, and attributes which a staff member must have to be effective within the UNHCR—both at headquarters and in the field.

These core values enable the UNHCR staff to align individual performance with overall agency strategy, as well as provide a clear framework for personal development:

- Commitment to humanitarian principles and to the UNHCR needs, priorities, goals, and values
- Ability to adapt to and work effectively in a variety of situations; and the flexibility to cope with unforeseen or unexpected events
- Ability to work effectively with colleagues from different backgrounds and cultures to achieve shared goals and optimize results
- Ability to display initiative and the determination to achieve results and to improve personal performance
- Ability to listen to—and understand—what people are trying to communicate; and the ability to express oneself in a clear and concise way
- Ability to demonstrate appropriate behavior in both professional and personal situations, as well as self-control, perseverance, and resilience

Defining core competencies is difficult. It takes hundreds of man-hours to secure ownership across a widely dispersed organization like the UNHCR. On the other hand, a Career Management System has tremendous value in terms of encouraging cohesiveness, open communications, mutual trust, and delineating authority where it was not clarified before.

In any organization where the headquarters is removed from the action, these core values form the glue that binds field workers with headquarters staff. This policy expresses the one overriding reality that recognition and promotion will go to those who are predominantly successful in the field, not to those who stalk the apparent corridors of power in Geneva.

Another important action in recent years has been the formulation of the managerial competencies appropriate to the UNHCR's mission, its management ethos, and style. These managerial skills drive home the importance which the UNHCR places on an individual's capacity for self-development and for developing the potential of others:

- Ability to develop and communicate in a clear strategic direction
- Ability to carry out the organization's vision, to manage change, to make timely decisions and be accountable for them, and to build, motivate, and lead a team
- Ability to create consensus with staff on objectives and competencies needed to achieve an overall plan, and to provide them with effective feedback on their performance
- Ability to provide effective coaching and to encourage staff development
- Ability to plan and use resources in accordance with guidelines and delegated accountability
- Ability to identify and understand relationships, constraints, and pressures affecting others, especially refugees

The ultimate goal of listing such managerial skills is to drive home the importance that the organization places on an individual's capacity for self-development and for developing the potential of others. Today, senior management at the UNHCR must demonstrate their continuing growth as managers and leaders, and they are all expected to set an example by undertaking management training.

The core competencies provide a written expression of the UNHCR's values and its underlying cohesion. But the managerial competencies promote true leadership by encouraging staff members to become models that exemplify those core values.

Since the office of the high commissioner is a political appointment by the General Assembly, I will have no hand in selecting my successor. However, I hope to leave behind an important legacy—a career system that recognizes the inherent diversity at the UN and seeks to leverage that diversity for excellence. ■

## Online Resources

- **Featured company**
  UN High Commissioner for Refugees
  http://www.unhcr.ch

- **Related articles**
  "Mervyn's Calls in the SWAT Team"
  By Peter Carbonara
  How does a retailing giant become faster and more flexible? By assembling a group of organizational commandos.
  http://www.fastcompany.com/online/14/swat.html

  "The Sacred and the Mundane"
  By Jeffrey L. Seglin
  Originally, icons were small paintings of saints' likenesses that were used to bring blessings to those who held them. Today the icons of business serve a similar, if more secular, purpose.
  http://www.inc.com/articles/details/0,,ART19017,00.html

# PART 3
# THE ENTREPRENEURIAL SPIRIT

# Japanese-Style Entrepreneurship

*Masayoshi Son*

*CEO and Founder, Softbank Corporation*

*Japan*

"For high-tech ventures, there are no footprints left by anyone else. You have to think and act as you think."

**Masayoshi Son**

The world of Japanese business, according to conventional thinking, consists of huge manufacturing corporations, tightly interwoven corporate families, and hordes of lifetime employees working as devoted company salarymen. Today, there is another world emerging—one of high-tech start-ups begun by young entrepreneurs who contribute their fresh global outlook and new generational attitudes to the traditional world of Japanese business. Masayoshi Son, 43, founder, president, and CEO of Softbank Corporation of Tokyo, exemplifies this new Japanese-style entrepreneurship.

Born in Japan of Korean heritage, Son attended high school in the United States—graduating in two weeks—and then went on to graduate from the University of California, Berkeley, where he started several businesses. At the age of 20, he used his technological skills to invent and patent a device he sold to Sharp Corporation for US$1 million. He returned to Japan in 1981 and, a year and a half later, started Softbank.

Today, Softbank is a leading provider of information and distribution services for the digital information industry, thanks to Son's aggressive investments in a variety of computer-related ventures. In addition to being Japan's largest distributor of packaged software and hardware, the company has stakes in 300 Internet-related companies, including E-Trade, Yahoo, and GeoCities, that span online book sales and financial services, reports *The Industry Standard*.

In this article, the competitive and self-made billionaire describes the beginnings of his empire.

I n 1981, I wanted to start my own company when I came back to Japan. So for a year and a half, I made business plans. I came up with 40 new business ideas, from creating software to setting up hospital chains. Then I had about 25 success measures that I used to decide which idea to pursue.

One success measure was that I should fall in love with a particular business for the next 50 years at least. Very often, people get excited for the first few years, and then they get tired of the business. I wanted to choose one that I would feel more excited about as the years passed.

Another factor was that the business should be unique. I didn't want anyone else doing exactly the same thing. A third was that within ten years I wanted to be the number one in that particular business where the business category itself would be growing for the next 30 to 50 years. I didn't want to choose a sinking ship.

I had those 25 measures and 40 new ideas. I took a big sheet of paper, drew a matrix, and put down scores and comments for each. Then I picked the best one, which turned out to be the personal computer software business. That was the start of Softbank.

In 1981, it wasn't obvious that software was the right industry. The PC was only a toy then. There was some hardware already made in Japan, but there was almost no software.

## A Matchmaking Mistake

When Softbank was only two or three months old, I decided that I needed to show the end users and dealers what software was available in Japan. There was a consumer electronics show in Tokyo, and I reserved the largest booth, the same size as Sony, Matsushita, and Toshiba. Then I called all the software vendors I could find, maybe just a dozen at that time. I told them that I had the space and I was going to prepare the flyers, displays, a model PC, and I was going to pay for everything. I told them, you, guys, can be in my booth for free. They all said, how can you do that? How can you make money doing that?

They had the software, but they didn't have the money to show it to anybody else. I had a little money, but I didn't have products to sell. And there were so many PC dealers who had hardware but no software. So, I thought, matchmaking was needed. At the consumer electronics show, I had a huge sign that said, "Now the revolution has come for software distribution for PCs." My booth was always packed with people. And they all said how good it was.

My plan was that some people would sign up to establish outlets and others would order software through Softbank. In fact, I got almost nothing. Nobody signed up for a dealership and I sold very few software products. Actually, most of the software vendors who occupied the booth would tell people, if you can't make up your mind today, call me directly if you decide to buy my software. So I was cut out of the deal completely. I probably made back one-twentieth of the cost of the booth.

After that, many people were laughing at me. They said, that guy's nice, but dumb. I said, OK, I'm dumb. But I'm going to keep at it, and someday, somebody will find out what I can do and what real software distribution means.

## My First Big Break

One person did call me from Osaka a few weeks after the show. He said, we're starting a big PC shop, and we need software. Please come and talk to me. I said, sorry but I'm too busy to make the trip right now. Actually, I wasn't busy. But I didn't have the money to go to Osaka.

He said, my company's name is Joshin Denki. Have you heard of us? I didn't know the company. It turns out it's the third largest home electronics dealer in Japan.

He said, please ask Sharp, ask Matsushita who we are. If you make up your mind to come to Osaka, we'd be happy to see you. So I called up Sharp because of my previous relationship with them when I was at Berkeley. They said, Joshin Denki called you! You should go to Osaka right away!

That afternoon, the person from Joshin Denki called me again. He said, you were too busy to come to Osaka. It's completely by chance, but tomorrow our president is going to Tokyo.

The next day the president, who told me he had come all the way to Tokyo just to see me, arrived. The company had started a big computer shop two weeks before, and it needed software. It already had some software and a direct channel with some vendors. But it wanted more.

I told him, if you want to do business with me, you'll have to discontinue all the relationships you've already formed. That's probably against your business ethics, but if you want to succeed with PCs in Japan, you should do business my way. He asked me, how much capital do you have? What kind of business experience do you have?

I told him, I have very little money and business experience. But I do have the greatest desire to succeed.

I said, you have already been purchasing some PC software and have more experience at this than I do. But in addition to purchasing PC software and hardware, you also purchase home electronics products, refrigerators, televisions, VCRs. I will dedicate all my time and effort to PC software only. Several months from now, who do you think will be more of a specialist in this business? If you want to be the number one PC dealer in Japan, you have to find the number one guy in software distribution. That's me.

He said, wow, you're an interesting guy! And he gave me exclusive purchasing rights for all the PC software for Joshin Denki. Joshin Denki had the biggest store specializing in PCs in Japan.

After I got Joshin Denki, I went to many department stores and electronic shops. Have you seen Joshin Denki? They're the largest PC dealer in Japan now. And do you know why they're so successful? Because they have the software! And I have the exclusive on that software. So if you want to succeed, please talk to me. And they all opened accounts with me very quickly. In one month, I got most of the biggest dealers in Japan as my customers.

Before I got Joshin Denki, I had almost no sales. Then right after I got Joshin Denki, I got about US$150,000 in sales to them. The next month, I started to do business with many other stores and that amount doubled. The next month, a 50% increase. And the next month. In one year, my monthly revenues went from about US$10,000 to US$2.3 million.

To make sales grow that quickly, one of the first things I did was to expand the choice of software that Joshin Denki had. I told them, I'm going to get all the PC software that's available in Japan. I said, you shouldn't decide which software you're going to buy for your store. I'm going to decide everything.

The president of Joshin Denki said, all right, but if the products don't sell, we should be able to return them to you. I told him, no. I said, in your other stores you have neon signs and showcases. Those are expensive. But in a PC shop, a neon sign doesn't do any good. What matters is software.

Software is part of the decoration. Even if it doesn't sell, if you have every software package that's available in Japan, that sends an important message to the end users. It tells them this is the biggest software lineup in Japan.

The idea really worked. Many people came to the store just because they heard that every software product was available there.

**Early Successes**

You probably wonder what entrepreneurial experiences prepared me to start Softbank. When I was a student at Berkeley, I started my first business and even hired some of the professors to help me. Actually, while I was at Berkeley, I had 250 inventions that I wrote down in my "Invention Idea Notes." Then I picked one to develop a prototype and apply for a patent. I made close to US$1 million by selling the patent to Sharp.

I came up with the idea in 1977 or 1978. I looked through the faculty directory and I called a number of faculty members. I wanted to know who was the best professor in the microcomputer field. I finally found a couple of good people.

I went to see them and said, I have some ideas. This is my sketch of my new invention. Will you help me? At first they said no, but finally I found a few who were interested. I formed a project team with these professors. I told them, I don't have money now, but I will pay you, so please keep track of how many hours you work on this project. After I got the money from Sharp for the patent, I paid them all.

The product is now called the Sharp Wizard, but the prototype was mine. It's a calculator-sized computer that can do translations in eight languages, like a dictionary, and there now exist many applications and software for it.

## Starting a Business in Japan: The Pros and Cons

I thought about pursuing my entrepreneurial career in the United States. Many things argued in favor of my staying there. Of course, the entrepreneurial climate there is much more responsive to someone who's trying to start a business. There's more capital.

In the United States, there's not the negative perception of the entrepreneur that there is in Japan. In general, it's harder to be an entrepreneur in Japan than in the United States. Japanese banks will not loan money to you because they are more conservative. And because of the culture, it's harder to attract the best employees. They like to work for the big companies or for the government because Japan is a lifetime employment country.

Still, the more I thought about it, the more reasons I found for starting my company in Japan. I had a very long-term vision. I believed that someday I would have a global business and a very successful company. To do that, my headquarters should be in Japan.

It's more difficult to start a business there, but once I had the company, it would be easier to keep the loyalty of Japanese employees. Japanese workers work harder, tend to stay in a company for a long time, and work very hard to make continuous improvements. In America, the workers are more likely either to leave the company after a while or not to care about the company very much.

In the beginning, it was very hard for us to get the best employees. We had to advertise in the newspapers and magazines, and it was still very difficult. We had to hire ex-truck drivers and all kinds of people for jobs they had never done before.

But these employees were very devoted to the company. They said, now I can work in a high-tech company. My family is very happy. I don't want to lose my job. So I will do my best. I had employees who worked so hard, they stayed overnight, sleeping on the floor of the office for three months at a time. They would go back home for only three or four days in three months. They worked like hell. They actually added to the spirit of the company.

I think I became an entrepreneur rather than join a successful Japanese corporation because I had my way of doing business. Especially for high-tech ventures, there are no footprints left by anyone else. You have to think and act as you think. To do that, you have to start your own company.

But if you have your own company, you're an outsider in the Japanese business world. It's difficult. But that's life. ∎

---

Reprinted by permission of **Harvard Business Review**. From "Japanese-Style Entrepreneurship: An interview with Softbank's CEO, Masayoshi Son" by Alan M. Webber, January-February 1992 issue. ©1992 by the President and Fellows of Harvard College. All rights reserved.

The biographical sketch was drawn using the following sources:
Guth, Rob. "Softbank Bets On Net." *The Industry Standard:* July 15, 1999.
Weinberg, Neil. "Master of the Internet." *Forbes:* July 5, 1999.

## Online Resources

- **Featured company**
  Softbank Corporation
  http://www.softbank.co.jp/ir/index_e.html

- **Related articles**
  "Starting Your Business"
  From Lycos.com
  Many of us hear the siren song of small business. But of those who answer it, most don't succeed. Why? What separates those who succeed from those who fail? This article will take you through the process of starting a new business.
  http://www.lycos.com/business/cch/
  guidebook.html?lpv=1&docNumber=P01_0000

  "Web Rebels"
  By Chester Dawson
  The Internet is breeding a generation of entrepreneurs outside the confines of Japan Inc. These young, nimble risk-takers are leading an e-business boom that promises to shake up corporate Japan.
  http://203.105.48.72/9907_29/p08cover.html

# Starting Up in High Gear

## Vinod Khosla

*General Partner, Kleiner Perkins Caufield & Byers*
*United States*

"In most cases now, it's absurd for an entrepreneur to spend a lot of time creating a business plan. Now you have to change course all the time— you have to adapt, not plan."

**Vinod Khosla**

Vinod Khosla is one of Silicon Valley's hottest hands. Since joining venture capitalists Kleiner Perkins Caufield & Byers in 1986, he has helped steer companies like Amazon.com, Excite, Juniper Networks, and Cerent to success.

The 46-year-old Khosla is known for nurturing start-ups, not just spreading cash. His pet start-ups Cerent and Siara Systems, for instance, sold for US$11.2 billion combined in 1999. He attributes his success as a venture capitalist to his hands-on experience in running Sun Microsystems—which he co-founded at the ripe old age of 27—and his business philosophy.

"I don't like the phrase 'venture capitalist' because I am not in the financial business," Khosla says in an interview. "I am in the 'venture assistance' business. My goal is to be the best assistant there is for anybody trying to build a large technology-oriented company." As a result, he spends "less than 1%" of his time looking at the financial aspects of a deal and 90% in the process of building a company—investing time in strategy, building relationships, and recruiting talent.

To recharge his batteries, Khosla, a father of four, makes it a point to get home for dinner and spend time with his family. In a business where executives are lucky if they make it home five nights a month, he prides himself on meeting his goal to be home for dinner at least 25 nights a month.

In this wide-ranging article, the loquacious venture capitalist and accomplished entrepreneur shares his thoughts on the secrets of entrepreneurial success and the Internet's impact on business. He also offers some cautionary words to established companies looking to shift their businesses onto the Internet.

## A Changed Landscape

I 've been asked if the keys to success for entrepreneurs have changed much since I started Sun 20 years ago. My answer is yes and no. It has always taken a certain combination of fearlessness and naiveté to be a successful entrepreneur, and that hasn't changed.

A few years back, when I was learning how to hang-glide, I watched an instructional movie that ended with a dedication like this: "To those who dare to dream the dreams, and then are foolish enough to try to make those dreams come true." That's a perfect description of an entrepreneur. You have to have the big idea, but you also have to be foolish enough to believe you can pull it off.

When we started Sun, if we had had any idea how hard it was to build a computer company, we never would have tried. We were in our 20s, and we had no clue about the challenges we were facing. We just plowed ahead. Each obstacle became something new to conquer. All entrepreneurs are like that, I think.

What has changed, though, is the landscape in which entrepreneurs operate. Everything moves much faster now, which means there's a lot less room for error. In the early 1980s, it didn't matter to IBM what we were doing at Sun—we were just a sneaky little start-up. Even when our revenues had reached US$100 million, we were nothing next to IBM's billions, and they couldn't be bothered to pay attention to us.

Back then, you had miles of runway before you showed up on the radar screens of large companies. That's not the case today. Amazon may have flown under Barnes & Noble's radar, but even Amazon had a much shorter free ride than we did at Sun. Now you have almost no time before you're under attack.

The notion that entrepreneurs have to spend a lot of time creating business plans has always seemed silly to me, but now in most cases it's completely absurd. In the past, you might have been able to write a business plan that could last a year or two before you had to change it. Now you have to change course all the time—you have to adapt, not plan.

The best you can do, I think, is have a sense of direction—an intuition about where the big opportunities are. Sure, I want to know that the management team and the entrepreneurs are capable of coming up with a strategy—but I now view that process as a discovery process, a way to hone ideas, rather than as a planning process.

## Alternating Between Greed and Fear

The rush to capitalize on Internet opportunities has set off a flood of venture financing. According to one study, more than US$14 billion in venture capital was invested in the fourth quarter of 1999—a fourfold increase over the year before.

I'm a bit concerned that that there's too much money out there. What's positive about it is that every conceivable economic experiment is being tried. All that cash is driving enormous innovation everywhere in business, and that's one of the fundamental strengths of the U.S. economy right now.

The dark side is that we're very much in a greed cycle. As we make this transition to a new economy, we're going to alternate between greed and fear, and greed holds sway right now. On a macro level, we can see the greed in the stock market. Over the long run, people who invest in the tech sector will earn great returns because the winners will be big winners.

But at the moment I'd say about 90% of the public companies in the sector are overvalued. We'll see a great deal of volatility in stock valuations for some time. The danger is that when the price corrections happen, we'll overreact on the fear side. Investment will dry up and the pace of experimentation will severely slow, putting the health of the overall economy at risk.

What concerns me even more, though, is the effect of the current greed cycle on entrepreneurs and their infant businesses. Today, if you have a plan for new business, you circulate it in the venture community and you get funded in a week. What you don't get is an honest, painstaking critique.

What are the downsides in your plan? What are the weak links? The strengths of your idea get a lot of attention, but the weaknesses get ignored—and ultimately it's the weakness of your plan that will kill you. A start-up is only as strong as its weakest link.

So I think the venture community is doing a disservice to entrepreneurs by funding them without forcing them to undergo a tough, critical examination. In the long run, it cripples new businesses.

Take the issue of talent, which is the most critical issue any start-up faces. Usually an entrepreneurial team has only one real skill set—they're great technologists or they're great marketers. When the venture process works well, the VCs help the entrepreneurs build the complete team. Without the full team, you can have early success, but after that things start to break down.

The lack of managerial skills, for instance, starts to foreclose further growth—and you can't add those skills later, because the top talent isn't going to want to join your company once it's gone public. As a result, great ideas never reach their full potential.

Frankly, the velocity of money is so high now, it's getting ugly. Too many people have too mercenary an attitude. When companies like Intel and Oracle and Apple and Sun got started, it wasn't about money. It was about passion, vision, and the desire to create something new that would have a lasting impact on people and the economy. The financial rewards flowed from that bigger vision.

There are still entrepreneurs who are driven by passion, but I fear that many of them—and many of their backers—are more focused on the big payoff. It's distasteful to see this sort of money grab.

## Overturning Basic Assumptions

Let's shift from start-ups to incumbents. It's been so hard for many established companies to adapt to the Internet for a number of reasons. One of the most important is that their top executives still tend to think of technology as a tool. Back when I was in business school, we were taught that first you develop your strategy and then you pick your tools—and technology was just one among many.

But now technology is a driver of business strategy. The answers to questions like "What business model makes sense?" and "What strategy makes sense?" are now a function of your assumptions about where technology is headed. And inside your company, your technology architecture determines how you procure supplies, provide customer support, configure your products, manage your sales channel—everything.

It's naive to think of a Web site as an "Internet strategy." The Internet us causing a complete overhaul of all aspects of business. It means new business models and new sources of competitive advantage. It demands new assets and different strategies.

As the speed of business picks up, we're seeing other basic assumptions about strategy being overturned as well. Think about the concept of scale, for instance. It used to be that the bigger you got, the lower your costs were and the better you did. Economies of scale were everything.

Of course, being big also meant that you were less able to adapt to change, but that didn't matter much because the rate of change was fairly low. You could get McKinsey to give you a new strategy every five years. Being big and slow was better than being small and nimble. That's turning around. The rate of change has become so high that the drawbacks of scale are outweighing the benefits. We're seeing diseconomies of scale.

A similar thing is happening with business processes. It used to be that the best companies had well-documented, state-of-the-art processes that all their employees knew and followed. Everything they did was carefully planned. But now, with decision-making time shrinking rapidly, the slowness of highly planned processes is a big disadvantage.

I'll use an example from the late 1980s. IBM had a great product-planning process, and they applied it to the first few laptops they developed. Following the process, they methodically researched every element of those machines. The laptops were beautifully designed. Unfortunately, they never got to market. By the time IBM finished the development process, the products were out-of-date. We're seeing this problem all over the place today: great processes that are completely unsuited to the new pace of business.

Yesterday, you optimized your business for cost and performance. Today, you have to optimize for flexibility and adaptability. Change is continuous now; it's not a discrete event anymore.

### Shake-up Time

That's a pretty scary thought if you're a big company that has spent all its time building up scale advantages and optimizing its processes. It's a very scary thought if you're unwilling or unsuited to change.

Large traditional companies are unsuited to the new environment for a host of reasons. First, they tend to be risk-averse, which is a big liability. There's so much experimentation going on right now that avoiding risk is the biggest risk you can take.

Second, they're too hierarchical in the way they communicate. Information moves slowly, and they just don't have the free flow of ideas that you need to succeed. Some hierarchy is necessary in decision making, but it should not extend to the flow of information.

Third, they don't have the right talent. When you can no longer depend on process and planning, instinct becomes very important. But big companies have never rewarded people for making gut calls, so over time they've bred the instinct out of their organizations. And it's very hard to teach instinct. Process can be taught, but to get good instinct you really have to bring in new people, create a new gene pool.

One CEO recently said to me, "I hope 30% of my senior managers are not here this time next year." That's a harsh thought, but it's a necessary thought. This isn't "be nice" time—it's shake-up time. If you don't make the hard decisions now, the best talent will continue to flow to start-ups.

In the end, though, it's not the big things that are going to kill you, it's the accumulation of little things. Most companies always do the top three or four critical things right. They start a Web site, they do the stuff that Bain and BCG tell them to. The problem is, everyone gets those things right. Its the micro decisions—the thousands of little decisions that a company makes every day—that are hard to get right.

What ad agency do you pick? Which engineer do you hire? The little things separate the dot.coms from the incumbents. A new company has no baggage. It can rethink everything from scratch and tune every decision to the new realities of communications and computing. But in a big company, the whole infrastructure and culture acts like gravity, pulling you back to where you started.

When I have some young entrepreneurs stepping up to bat against Wal-Mart or Ford or AT&T, I tell them, "Guys, you're gonna go up to the plate with two strikes against you. There are a lot of things you don't have—like brand, like distribution, like scale, like staying power. So you can't make too many mistakes. But you've got one huge advantage: Your competition has minor-league pitchers."

It's not that the big guys' assets arent valuable. They are. If they could apply the instincts of an entrepreneur to those assets, the big guys would be unbeatable. But that almost never happens because big companies, whatever they might say, aren't open to change. ∎

---

Reprinted by permission of **Harvard Business Review**. From "Starting Up in High Gear: An Interview with Venture Capitalist Vinod Khosla" by David Champion and Nicholas G. Carr, July-August 2000 issue. Copyright 2000 by the President and Fellows of Harvard College. All rights reserved.

The biographical sketch was drawn using the following sources:
Sharma, Mona. "The Venture Grandmaster." *Silicon India*: August 1997.
"The e.biz 25: Masters of the Web World." *Business Week*: May 15, 2000.

# Online Resources

• **Featured company**
Kleiner Perkins Caufield & Byers
http://www.kpcb.com/

• **Related articles**
"Eyes Wide Open"
By Steven C. Currall
The tremendous value Wall Street places on e-commerce and dot.com start-ups has many in the Fortune 500 structuring their e-commerce efforts along the organizational lines of the Silicon Valley start-up. Yet start-ups, notwithstanding all their advantages, often make flawed business decisions.
http://www2.cio.com/archive/041500_new_content.html

"Unbundling the Corporation"
By John Hagel III and Marc Singer
The forces that fractured the computer industry are bearing down on all industries. In the face of changing interaction costs and the new economics of electronic networks, companies must ask themselves the most basic of all questions: What business are we in?
http://mckinseyquarterly.com/article_page.asp?articlenum=857

# Fast, Global, and Entrepreneurial: Supply Chain Management, Hong Kong Style

*Victor Fung*

*Chairman, Li & Fung*

*Hong Kong SAR*

"We are a smokeless factory."

**Victor Fung**

Victor Fung is no low-margin Hong Kong middleman. At Li & Fung, the export trading company which he chairs, sales rose 14% in 1999 to US$21 billion, and profits were US$74 million—up 26%.

Li & Fung is an innovator in the development of supply chain management. On behalf of its customers, primarily American and European retailers, it works with an ever-expanding network of thousands of suppliers around the globe, sourcing clothing and other consumer goods ranging from fashion accessories to luggage. But the trading company is more than a matchmaker; it provides clients with a full package of services—from buying raw materials to planning production and monitoring manufacturing—for which it earns commissions of 7% to 12% on the value of each order it fills.

That's a huge expansion on the role of the original Li & Fung, which was founded in 1906 by Fung patriarch, Fung Pak-liu, to bring goods in and out of southern China. In the early 1970s, Victor, who was teaching at the Harvard Business School, and his younger brother, William, then a newly minted Harvard MBA, were called home from the United States by their father to breathe new life into the company. Today, the brainy brothers make a formidable team: While 55-year-old Victor is the visionary, 52-year-old William, as Li & Fung's group managing director, is responsible for day-to-day operations. In addition, Victor is also chairman of the Hong Kong Trade Development Council and Prudential Asia Investments Ltd.

The Fungs built Hong Kong's leading trading company by leading Li & Fung through a series of transformations. In the process, they have created a new kind of multinational, one that remains entrepreneurial despite its growing size and scope.

*In this article, Victor Fung describes how the company made the transition from being a buying agent to a supply chain manager, from the old economy to the new, and from a traditional Chinese family conglomerate to an innovative public company.*

W hen my grandfather started the company 93 years ago, his "value added" was that he spoke English. No one at the Chinese factories spoke English and the American merchants spoke no Chinese. As an interpreter, my grandfather's commission was 15%.

Continuing through my father's generation, Li & Fung was basically a broker, charging a fee to put buyers and sellers together. However, as an intermediary, the company was squeezed between the growing power of the buyers and the factories. Our margins slipped to 10%, then 5%, then 3%. When I returned to Hong Kong in 1976 after teaching at Harvard Business School, my friends warned me that in ten years buying agents like Li & Fung would be extinct.

My brother and I felt we could turn the business into something different, and so we took it through several stages of development. In the first stage, we acted as a regional sourcing agent and extended our geographic reach by establishing offices in Taiwan, Korea, and Singapore. We could then provide a package from the whole region rather than a single product from Hong Kong.

By working with a larger number of countries, we were able to assemble components. Say, I sell a tool kit to a major discount chain. I could buy the spanners from one country and the screwdrivers from another and put together a product package. That has some value in it—not great value, but some.

In the second stage, we delivered manufacturing programs. In the old model, the customer would say, "This is the item I want. Please go out and find the best place to buy it for me." The new model works this way: The Limited, one of our big customers, comes to us and says, "For next season, this is what we're thinking about—this look, these colors, these quantities. Can you come up with a production program?"

We then create an entire program for the season, specifying the product mix and the schedule. We work with factories to plan production so that we can ensure quality and on-time delivery.

This strategy carried us through the 1980s, but that decade brought us a new challenge—and led to our third stage. As the Asian tigers emerged, Hong Kong became an increasingly expensive place to manufacture. What saved us was that China began to open up to trade, allowing Hong Kong to move the labor-intensive portion of production across the border into southern China.

So, for transistor radios, we created little kits—plastic bags filled with all the components needed to build a radio. Then we shipped the kits to China for assembly. After the labor-intensive work was completed, the finished goods came back to Hong Kong for final testing and inspection.

## A Quantum Leap

Breaking up the value chain as we did was a novel concept at the time. We call it "dispersed manufacturing." This method of manufacturing soon spread to other industries, transforming Hong Kong's economy. Between 1979 and 1997, Hong Kong's position as a trading entity moved from number 21 in the world to number 8. All our manufacturing moved into China, and Hong Kong became a huge service economy with 84% of its gross domestic product coming from services.

Managing dispersed production was a real breakthrough. It forced us to get smart not only about logistics and transportation but also about dissecting the value chain.

Because not everything is done under one roof, it took a real change of mindset. But once we figured out how to do it, it became clear that our reach should extend beyond southern China. Our thinking was, for example, if wages were lower farther inland, let's go there. And so we began what has turned into a constant search for new and better sources of supply.

Li & Fung made a quantum leap in 1995. We nearly doubled our size and extended our geographic scope by acquiring Inchcape Buying Services (now called Dodwell), a large British *hong* with an established network of offices in India, Pakistan, Bangladesh, and Sri Lanka. The acquisition also brought with it a European customer base that complemented Li & Fung's predominantly American base.

## Pulling the Value Chain Apart

This Hong Kong model of borderless manufacturing has become a new paradigm for Asia. But the region is still very dependent on the ultimate sources of demand, which are in North America and Western Europe. They start the whole cycle going.

When we get a typical order, say, an order from a European retailer to produce 10,000 garments, it's not a simple matter of our Korean office sourcing Korean products or our Indonesian office sourcing Indonesian products. For this customer, we might decide to buy yarn from a Korean producer but have it woven and dyed in Taiwan. So we pick the yarn and ship it to Taiwan.

The Japanese have the best zippers and buttons, but they manufacture them mostly in China. So we order the right zippers from their Chinese plants. Then we determine that, because of quotas and labor conditions, the best place to make the garments is Thailand. So we ship everything there. And because the customer needs quick delivery, we may divide the order across five factories in Thailand. Effectively, we are customizing the value chain to best meet the customer's needs.

Five weeks after we have received the order, 10,000 garments arrive on the shelves in Europe, all looking like they came from one factory. Just think about the logistics and the coordination.

This is a new type of value added, a truly global product that has never been seen before. The label may say "Made in Thailand" but it's not a Thai product. We're pulling apart the value chain and optimizing each step—and we're doing it globally.

Not only do the benefits outweigh the costs of logistics and transportation, but the higher value added also allows us to charge more for our services. We deliver a sophisticated product and we deliver it fast. If you talk to the big global consumer-products companies, they are all moving in this direction—toward being best on a global scale.

Today, assembly is the easy part. The hard part is managing your suppliers and the flow of parts. In retailing, these changes are producing a revolution. For the first time, retailers are really creating products, not just sitting in their offices with salesman after salesman showing them samples. Instead, retailers are now managing suppliers through us and are even reaching down to their suppliers' suppliers. Eventually that translates into much better management of inventories and lower markdowns in the stores.

Companies in consumer-driven, fast-moving markets face the problem of obsolete inventory with a vengeance. If you can shorten your buying cycle from three months to five weeks, for example, what you are gaining is eight weeks to develop a better sense of where the market is heading. And so you will end up with substantial savings in inventory markdowns at the end of the selling season.

Good supply-chain management strips away time and cost from product delivery cycles. Our customers have become more fashion-driven, working with six or seven seasons a year instead of just two or three. Once you move to shorter product cycles, the problem of obsolete inventory increases dramatically. Other businesses are facing the same kind of pressure. With customer tastes changing rapidly and markets segmenting into narrower niches, it's not just fashion products that are becoming increasingly time-sensitive.

Supply-chain management is about buying the right things and shortening the delivery cycles. It requires "reaching into the suppliers" to ensure that certain things happen on time and at the right level of quality.

Here's an example of how you reach into the supply chain to shorten the buying cycle: Think about what happens when you outsource manufacturing. The easy approach is to place an order for finished goods and let the supplier worry about contracting for the raw materials like fabric and yarn. But a single factory is relatively small and doesn't have much buying power; that is, it is too small to demand faster deliveries from its suppliers.

## Tackling the "Soft US$3"

We come in and look at the whole supply chain. We know The Limited is going to order 100,000 garments, but we don't know the style or the colors yet. The buyer will tell us that five weeks before delivery. The trust between us and our supply network means that we can reserve undyed yarn from the yarn supplier. I can lock up capacity at the mills for the weaving and dying with the promise that they'll get an order of a specified size; five weeks before delivery, we will let them know what colors we want. Then I say the same thing to the factories, "I don't know the product specs yet, but I have organized the colors and the fabric and the trim for you, and they'll be delivered to you on this date and you'll have three weeks to produce so many garments."

It would be easier to let the factories worry about securing their own fabric and trim. But then the order would take three months, not five weeks. So to shrink the delivery cycle, I go upstream to organize production. And the shorter production time lets the retailer hold off before having to commit to a fashion trend. It's all about flexibility, response time, small production runs, small minimum-order quantities, and the ability to shift direction as the trends move.

It is also about cost. At Li & Fung, we think about supply chain management as "tackling the soft US$3" in the cost structure. This means that if a typical consumer product leaves the factory at a price of US$1, it will invariably end up on retail shelves at US$4. Now, you can try to squeeze the cost of production down 10 cents or 20 cents per product, but there's not a lot of fat left. It's better to look at the cost that is spread throughout the distribution channels—the soft US$3. It offers a bigger target and it's a much easier place to effect savings for our customers.

For example, shippers always want to fill a container to capacity. And if all you care about is the cost of shipping, there's no question you should fill the containers. But if you think instead of the whole value chain as a system, and you're trying to lower the total cost and not just one piece of it, then it may be smarter not to fill the containers.

Let's say you want to distribute an assortment of ten products, each manufactured by a different factory, to ten distribution centers. The standard practice would be for each factory to ship full containers of its product. So those ten containers would have to go to a consolidator, who would unpack and repack all ten containers before shipping the assortment to the distribution centers.

Now, suppose instead that you move one container from factory to factory and get each factory to fill just one-tenth of the container. Then you ship it with the assortment the customer needs directly to the distribution center. The shipping cost will be greater. But the total systems cost could be lower because you've eliminated the consolidator altogether.

## Managing a Million Workers

So when you talk about organizing the value chain, what you do goes well beyond simply contracting for other people's services or inspecting their work. It sounds like the value you add extends almost to the point where you're providing management expertise to your supply network.

In a sense, we are a smokeless factory. We do design. We buy the raw materials. We have factory managers, people who plan production and balance the lines. We inspect production. But we don't manage the workers and we don't own the factories.[1]

---

[1] In 1999, the trading company broke its own commndment not to own factories. While Li & Fung (Trading) has prospered through strict adherence to this rule, preferring to keep an eye on production through regular visits to plants to contact, Li & Fung (Distribution), on the other hand, owns eight factories and manages 6,000 employees.

In this case, it seems rules were made to be broken. As the Fungs try to transform Li & Fung (Distribution) from a grab bag of businesses into a lean distribution machine, they are concentrating on making life easier for multinationals. If a shampoo maker wants to sell to Asia, for instance, Li & Fung can now offer to blend the active ingredients at one of its factories, sell the product to retailers, and deliver it to them.

Think about the scope of what we do. We work with about 7,500 suppliers in more than 26 countries. If the average factory has 200 workers, then in effect there are more than a million workers engaged on behalf of our customers. That's why our policy is not to own any portion of the value chain that deals with running factories. Managing a million workers would be a colossal undertaking. We'd lose all flexibility. So we deliberately leave that management challenge to the individual entrepreneurs we contract with.

If we don't own factories, can we say we are in manufacturing? Absolutely. Because, of the 15 steps in the manufacturing value chain, we probably do ten.

## Little "John Waynes"

The way Li & Fung is organized is unusual in the industry. Let me describe the link between our organization and our strategy.

Just about every company I know says that it is customer-focused. Usually, this means that it designs key systems that fit most of its customers, they hope, most of the time. Here, we do something different: We organize for the customer. Almost all the large trading companies with extensive networks of suppliers are organized geographically, with the country units as their profit centers. As a result, their country units are competing against one another for business.

Our basic operating unit is the division. Whenever possible, we will focus an entire division on serving one customer. We may serve smaller customers through a division structured around a group of customers with similar needs. This structuring of the organization around customers is very important—remember that what we do is close to creating a customized value chain for every customer order.

So, customer-focused divisions are the building blocks of our organization, and we keep them small and entrepreneurial. They do anywhere from US$20 million to US$50 million of business. Each is run by a lead entrepreneur—we sometimes call them "little John Waynes" because the image of a guy standing in the middle of the wagon train, shooting at all the bad guys, seems to fit.

The idea is to create small units dedicated to taking care of one customer, and to have one person running a unit like he or she would his or her own company. We hire people whose main alternative would be to run their own business. We provide them with the financial resources and the administrative support of a big organization, but we give them a great deal of autonomy. All the merchandising decisions that go into coordinating a production program for the customer are made at the division-head level. For the creative parts of the business, we want entrepreneurial behavior, so we give people considerable operating freedom.

To motivate the division leaders, we rely on substantial financial incentives by tying their compensation directly to the unit's bottom line. There's no cap on bonuses: we want entrepreneurs who are motivated to move heaven and earth for the customer.

Trading companies can be run effectively only when they are small. By making small units the heart of our company, we have been able to grow rapidly without becoming bureaucratic. Today, we have about 60 divisions. We think of them as a portfolio that we can create and collapse, almost at will. As the market changes, our organization can adjust immediately.

What role, then, does the corporate center play? When it comes to financial controls and operating procedures, we centralize and manage tightly. Li & Fung has a standardized, fully computerized operating system for executing and tracking orders, and everyone in the company uses the system.

We also keep very tight control of working capital. Inventory is the root of all evil. So it's a word we don't tolerate around here. All cash flow is managed centrally through Hong Kong. All letters of credit, for example, come to Hong Kong for approval and are then re-issued by the central office. That means we are guaranteed payment before we execute an order.

We've grown substantially both in size and in geographic scope. Since 1993, we've changed from a Hong Kong-based Chinese company that was

99.5% Chinese and probably 80% Hong Kong Chinese into a truly regional multinational with offices in 30 countries.

As we spread out geographically, to hold the organization together, the company is managed on a day-to-day basis by the product group managers. Along with the top management, they form what we call the policy committee, which consists of about 30 people. We meet once every five to six weeks. People fly in from around the region to discuss policies. Consider, for example, the topic of compliance, or ethical sourcing. How do we make sure our suppliers are doing the right thing—by our customers' standards and our own—when it comes to issues such as child labor, environmental protection, and country-of-origin regulations?

The committee of 30 not only shapes our policies but also translates them into operating procedures which we think will be effective in the field. They then become a vehicle for implementing what we've agreed on when they return to their divisions.

### Old Relationships, New Technology

There are few businesses as old as trading. Yet the essence of what we do at Li & Fung—managing information and relationships—sounds like a good description of the information economy. At one level, Li & Fung is an information node, flipping information between our 350 customers and our 7,500 suppliers.

But even in the information age, the old relationships, the old values, still matter. I think they matter in our dealings with suppliers, with customers, and with our own staff.

Right now, we're so big, three of our divisions could be scheduling work with the same factory. So I'm creating a database to track systematically all our supplier relationships. One of my colleagues said, "We'd better guard that with our lives, because if somebody ever got into our system, he could steal one of the company's greatest assets." I'm not so worried. Someone might steal our database, but when he calls up a supplier, he doesn't have the long relationship with the supplier that Li & Fung has.

I think there is a similar traditional dimension to our customer relationships. In the old days, my father used to read every telex from customers. That made a huge difference in a business where a detail as small as the wrong zipper color could lead to disastrous delays for customers. Today, William and I continue to read faxes from customers—not every one, but enough to keep us in personal touch with our customers and our operations on a daily basis.

As we have transformed a family business into a modern one, we have tried to preserve the best of what my father and grandfather created. There is a family feeling in the company that's difficult to describe. We don't care much for titles and hierarchy. We hold on to our wish to preserve the intimacies that have been at the heart of our most successful relationships. If I had to capture it in one phrase, it would be this: Think like a big company, act like a small one. ■

---

The biographical sketch was drawn using the following source:

The correspondents and editors of *Business Week*. "The Stars of Asia: 50 Leaders at the Forefront of Change." *Business Week*: July 3, 2000.

# Online Resources

- **Featured companies**
  Hong Kong Trade Development Council
  http://www.tdc.org.hk/

  Li & Fung
  http://www.lifung.com

- **Related article**
  "Masters of the Trade"
  By Joanna Slater with Eriko Amaha
  Victor and William Fung built one of Asia's most successful trading houses by reacting quickly to changes in the way their multinational clients do business. Now the big shift is from sourcing in Asia to selling there, too.
  http://203.105.48.72/9907_22/p10cover.html

- **Related Web site**
  Supply Chain Management Research Center
  Supply Chain Management is the science of optimizing—usually through the use of software—a company's methods of manufacturing, storing, and shipping the products it sells. CIO.com, the leading resource for information executives, offers a comprehensive list of supply chain resources, consultants, and books in its research center.
  http://www.cio.com/forums/scm/

# Lessons from a Master Entrepreneur

*William Heinecke*

*Chief Executive Officer, The Minor Group*
*Thailand*

"In business, decisions based on intuition are often superior to those based on analytical reasoning. You can pore over statistics, marketing reports, and spreadsheets, but sometimes you just have to trust your instincts."

**William Heinecke**

William Heinecke sits on top of a sprawling business empire. He owns controlling stakes in two companies—Royal Garden Resort, with its seven luxury hotels and two shopping malls, and Pizza Co., which owns franchises for Pizza Hut, the Swensen's and Dairy Queen ice-cream outlets, and Sizzler steakhouses scattered all over Thailand—and a third, Minor Corp., through his wholly owned Minor Holdings.

What ties these different businesses together? Entrepreneurial smarts. Heinecke, 51, is known for persuading the Thais to eat pizza, building luxury hotels and shopping malls where others feared to tread, and spotting trends and opportunities.

His entrepreneurial skills have enabled him not only to survive the economic turmoil of the past two years, but to prosper through a strategy of price-cutting and streamlining the two most important parts of his business empire: food and hotels. To survive, Heinecke's strategy was to keep old customers and bring in new ones at virtually any cost. It worked: 1998 was a record year for both Royal Garden Resort and for Pizza Co. The hotel business reported a net profit of 228 million baht in 1998, against a loss of 226 million baht in 1997. At the fast-food business, net profits rose to a record 178 million baht from 82 million baht in 1997.

Heinecke, who arrived in Bangkok in 1963 and started an advertising business with a US$1,200 loan when he was just 18, has distilled his hard-won insights into his best-selling book, *The Entrepreneur: 21 Golden Rules for the Global Business Manager*. In this excerpt, he elaborates on the importance of research, hiring smart employees, trusting one's intuition, and acting quickly in a crisis.

## Do Your Homework

Whether you are just starting out, looking to expand, or already control a number of businesses, a rule of successful entrepreneurship is, do your homework.

A lot of ideas can come from casual observation. The idea to set up Pizza Hut in Thailand came when I was sitting in a pizza restaurant in Manila in the late 1970s with a group of friends, and I was asked what business ideas might work in Thailand. "Look around you," I replied. We were in a Shakey's restaurant full of Filipinos and Westerners happily munching away at their pizzas.

The longer I thought about the idea, the more attractive it became. So I wrote Pizza Hut and told their representative I wanted to try the idea out with one restaurant. Our first restaurant was in Pattaya, 100 kilometers east of Bangkok. We figured that if the Thais didn't go for the pizza, there were always the Western tourists and U.S. navy personnel on R&R leave who flocked to the town.

I remember the place well—I had an apartment at the roof of the building and used to watch the passing crowds. We didn't make a huge profit, but we were intrigued to see that half of the customers were Thai. The next year we opened a second Pizza Hut in Bangkok. And then another, and another. Today, there are more than 100 Pizza Huts in Thailand.

The success of Pizza Hut proves that doing your homework can be a real education. When I was researching the project I was told that it would be unwise to start a pizza operation, because Thais don't like cheese, wouldn't eat pizza, and weren't ready for Western-style fast food.

But I introduced pizza at a time when many things were starting to change in Thailand. The middle class was growing quickly, and many Western ideas were being adopted. Younger people had more money in their pockets and were seeking greater lifestyle choices. Eating pizza in an air-conditioned, American-style restaurant became a perfect symbol of increasing purchasing power and changing consumer attitudes.

Here are some points to consider when doing your homework:

*Consider a franchise.* Franchising is perfect for the first-time entrepreneur, as agreements can be granted for a single store. The contract, normally for between 10 and 30 years, often has a development requirement, sales projections, and a time limit in which to achieve results.

There is another benefit: Franchises enable you to gain access to information and technology that you would otherwise have to spend a lot of money developing. This is a quick way to benchmark your business.

*Do your research.* Research comes in many forms and can start right at street level. When we research the location for a new Pizza Hut, we count the number of pedestrians and cars in the vicinity of the proposed restaurant.

Then we have a close look at the numbers. Are these the sort of people who are going to spend a lot of money? It's all very well having thousands of people who regularly use a ferry crossing, but are they thousands of people with no money to spend? As they used to say about China in the 1970s, a billion zeros equals zero.

Another method is simply to take a company you admire and see what it is doing well; you can call it piggyback research. What opportunities are being created? People have bought land in the vicinity of our hotels. Their thinking is that if we have got our sums right, the value of land is going to increase and business in the area will boom.

*Think laterally.* Identify complementary business opportunities that could stem from your initial idea. If you are going to build a hotel, why not include a shopping plaza to help offset the cost of the hotel? We have developed residential condominiums, shopping plazas, and office buildings to help increase the returns from our hotels. Our Pizza Huts and Swensen's are often located close by each other, so that we can use the same warehouses and delivery routes.

## Work with Other People's Brains

Whatever the enterprise, you must have the technical knowhow or be able to hire it. This is called working with other people's brains.

I learned advertising from David Ogilvy, one of the most inspirational figures in world advertising. His advice to me, which I've never forgotten, was always to hire people who were smarter than I was. If you keep hiring people who are smarter than you in important areas, you will build an organization that is very strong.

Furthermore, when hiring people, never let too much knowledge blot out the creative spark. Let me explain: Even an MBA has his limitations; he is an administrator, not an entrepreneur. The MBA's strength lies in his ability to preserve funds. The entrepreneur's strength lies in coming up with ideas that generate cash flow. The former focuses on *cost* centers, while the latter focuses on *profit* centers.

So embrace the specialist, but keep your creative juices flowing. You need each other.

I also think it is important to hire people you like working with. It makes the whole process much more enjoyable. Bill Bensley, who is in my view one of the world's great landscape architects, and John Lightbody, a brilliant interior designer, have worked on our hotel projects for many years. Our working relationships have blossomed into great friendships, ensuring that our hotels' garden and interior designs are considered among the best in the world.

If you work with people who are very bright in their own field and have diverse talents, you will develop a team of tremendous strength and depth. You will never regret the time you put into developing and working with great talent. It is people like these who will help make you a more successful entrepreneur.

**Trust Your Intuition**

I have always relied heavily on intuition, and most of the time it has paid dividends. For example, the idea to build a US$60-million shopping, entertainment, and hotel complex in Pattaya in 1991 raised many eyebrows and even a few laughs. Critics said that a new 300-room Royal Garden Resort and 50,000-square-meter Royal Garden Plaza shopping mall, including restaurants and the Ripley's Believe It Or Not!

Museum, would become expensive white elephants. After all, they said, Pattaya was famous for two things: prostitution and pollution. Red lights and raw sewage were unlikely to make a winning combination for such a big investment.

But I *knew* Pattaya. There was much more to the place than the seedy strip and a grubby beach. In terms of purchasing power, there wasn't any city in Thailand that compared. When people went to Pattaya, it was a spending experience. They wanted to be entertained, to eat, and to go shopping.

That was the pitch, but at first the critics seemed to be right. We began building the complex in 1991 and the timing couldn't have been worse. The Gulf War broke out, there was a coup in Thailand, and a global recession was starting to bite. Undeterred, we pressed on and by 1995 the Royal Garden Resort and Royal Garden Plaza were open for business.

Well, it worked. The hotel has been a huge success and, after a slow start, the retail space in the shopping plaza was fully rented out. Almost 10 million people now visit the plaza annually. As for Ripley's, within a couple of months 50,000 people a month were pouring through the doors.

It pays to dare to be different. So try to develop an awareness of your own intuition and learn to trust it.

## Act Quickly in a Crisis

On July 2, 1997, a series of events was set in motion that threatened to destroy everything I had built in Thailand. On that day, the Bank of Thailand revealed the horrible truth: Attempts to defend the baht had failed; the only option was to let the currency float.

For years, the baht had been one of the most stable currencies in Asia, barely budging far from 25 to the greenback. In January 1998 it hit 56. The Stock Exchange of Thailand Index fell from a peak of 1700 in the mid-1990s to below 250.

Before long the corporate landscape started to resemble an abattoir. Huge amounts of wealth were destroyed. Nobody had anticipated just how bad the crisis would get.

So what did we do? First, we looked at the bright side: We had repaid US$35 million of the group's U.S. dollar debt before the June 30 float of the baht.

Then, I instructed all our managers to take a hard look at their staff and remove the bottom 10%. At one of our restaurants that employed 20 people, we sacked the two poorest-performing employees and suffered no loss in service or efficiency.

We overhauled our pricing strategy in the restaurants. We knew that customers would have less money, so they would have to see great value before they would part with any of it.

When the crisis started in 1997, the cheapest pizza you could buy at Pizza Hut was 149 baht, which was around US$6. In July 1998, we dropped the price to 99 baht, which was less than US$3 at the exchange rates of the day. Our strategy was the same at Swensen's, where for a month we reduced prices to what they had been when we opened ten years earlier—12 baht (about 30 cents) per scoop of ice cream.

At both companies, we still made a profit and attracted swarms of customers. The result was that we emerged from the crisis with a greater market share in the new market where customers were more confident to spend and absorb price increases.

We closed down several non-core companies that were unprofitable. We also outsourced things like security and cleaning, and focused on what we did best. And we sold everything we could to raise cash. Then we hung on and tried to weather the storm.

In 1996, our companies made 300 million baht (over US$12 million). In 1997, we lost 1 billion baht (over US$30 million). But little by little, things started to turn around. As a result, 1998 was the best year in the history of our company; as a group, we made almost 500 million baht (around US$15 million).

We survived by following some basic rules: Always be positive. Your staff expects you to lead them when the going gets tough. And determine what your priorities are, keep your focus on them, and act quickly. ■

The biographical sketch was drawn using the following source:

Tasker, Rodney. "Home and Away." *Far Eastern Economic Review*: May 27, 1999.

## Online Resources

- **Related articles**

"Hiring Employees"

If you're one of those new small businesses that needs to hire employees, you have a daunting task ahead of you. Fortunately, there are some steps you can take to help you get just the right person and to save yourself some time in the process.

http://www.lycos.com/business/cch/
guidebook.html?lpv=1&docNumber=P05_0001

"True Grit"

By Edward O. Welles

Forget IQ. Forget EQ. It is the AQ—adversity quotient—of an individual or an organization that determines entrepreneurial success.

http://www.inc.com/incmagazine/article/
1,3654,ART19527_CNT53,00.html

"What's Your Intuition?"

By Bill Breen

Cognitive psychologist Gary Klein has studied people who make do-or-die decisions. His advice? Trust your instincts.

http://www.fastcompany.com/online/38/klein.html

# Creating a Poverty-Free World

## Muhammad Yunus

Founder and Managing Director, Grameen Bank
Bangladesh

"Poverty is not created by poor people. It is produced by our failure to create institutions to support human capabilities."

**Muhammad Yunus**

Muhammad Yunus, 61, is no ordinary banker, and not by any stretch of the imagination is Grameen—meaning Rural Bank—a conventional financial institution. It exists for one purpose: to turn into reality Yunus's philosophy of banking for the poor, offering them collateral-free loans rarely more than US$100, so they can lift themselves out of the mire of poverty.

Yunus—who pays himself a modest salary, wears simple clothes, and lives in a two-bedroom flat in Dhaka—has been helping the poor in his native Bangladesh for more than 20 years. But don't talk to him about charity. His 12,000-employee bank, which lends US$35 million every month, is a commercially profitable bank. More important, it saves borrowers' lives: About half of the borrowers rise above the poverty line within a decade of their first loan.

Part of Grameen's success can be attributed to its unique policies, which, Yunus explains, support and protect each borrower. Borrowers are required to form groups of five and meet weekly to discuss each other's businesses and to pre-approve one another's loan proposals. They decide how much to borrow for practically any income-generating activity—fish farming, basket making, or textile weaving—at 20% non-compound interest, repaid in 52 weekly installments. If one member falls behind on payments, no other group member may borrow until the debt is paid.

In this article, Yunus discusses how his ideas for microcredit first took shape, the fundamental premises which have hindered economists' efforts to solve the problem of poverty, and Grameen's moves into innovative "social consciousness-driven" businesses.

139

W hy we have so much poverty in the world is because we have not addressed the issue right. Poverty is not created by poor people or by the lack of demand for labor. It is created by our failure to create a theoretical framework, institutions, and policies to support human capabilities.

In 1971, I returned home to my newly independent country of Bangladesh after having received my doctorate in economics from Vanderbilt University in the United States. I joined Chittagong University as chairman of the economics department. I was full of optimism that good things would necessarily occur after such a terrible war. However, the euphoria of creating a dreamland for 75 million people died down rapidly as the economy took a nosedive, resulting in a famine in 1974.

All the brilliant theories I was teaching my students did not alleviate the starvation of millions of people. It became difficult for me to focus on the theories of classroom economics while, around me, my fellow human beings were dying. I wanted to understand the lives of poor people, to find out what had made them so vulnerable to famine.

I went into the village of Jobra, just outside of Chittagong University. I wanted to rid myself of the arrogance that accompanies a PhD: the tendency to view situations with a bird's-eye view. I attempted to obtain a worm's-eye view—to focus on one tiny problem and try to surmount it— a much more effective strategy because it is grounded in reality.

I met a woman in the village of Jobra, a bamboo weaver named Sufiya Khatun. She was a widow with two daughters. Sufiya made such beautiful bamboo stools, I thought that she must be making a decent amount of money. Imagine my shock when I discovered that she only earned two U.S. cents each day. Two cents!

The reason for this meager amount? Sufiya had to borrow the money at 10% interest from a local moneylender, who lent it to her on the condition that she sold the stools back to him at a price he set, at a measly profit.

I realized why this woman suffered: the cost of the bamboo was five taka, about 20 U.S. cents, but she lacked the start-up capital. It was so simple: all that was necessary was to lend Sufiya the five taka and her problem was solved.

Sufiya's predicament was prevalent among the stool-makers in the village of Jobra. What was the amount of working capital necessary to free them from the exploitation by traders and moneylenders? After a quick survey, we compiled a list of 42 people and the grand total came up to US$27.

For lack of US$27, 42 persons were spending their lives within a vicious cycle of poverty. And this was not a situation unique to the village of Jobra. In country after country, from Bolivia to the Philippines to South Africa, I had seen exactly the same phenomenon—hard-working people condemned to a life of misery because they lacked access to tiny amounts of capital. If it were possible to bring financial capital into the hands of the poor, there would be an opportunity for them to enjoy the fruits of their labor.

But in reality, the existing economic machinery is designed in such a way that the earnings of others can make a handful of people richer every day while, at the same time, turning a large number of people into paupers. At the heart of this economic machinery is the failure of economics as a social science.

Three fundamental assumptions have misled economists away from solving the problem of poverty: credit is a neutral tool; entrepreneurs belong to a select group of people; and capitalism is reliant upon maximizing profit.

## Credit Is a Neutral Tool

The poor are poor because they are not able to retain the genuine returns to their labor; they work for the benefit of someone who controls the capital. The poor have no control over capital. They do not inherit any capital, nor does anybody give them access to capital or credit.

Most economists have consistently failed to understand the social power of credit. Credit creates entitlement to resources. Consequently, credit creates economic power, which, in turn, creates social power.

Thus, the responsibility for deciding who will get credit, how much, and on what terms, is an important social question. A lending institution can make or break an entire segment of society by favoring or rejecting its members. Banks pronounced a death sentence on the poor with the announcement that the poor are not creditworthy.

In the village of Jobra, I lent US$27 of my own money to 42 people. After a few days, I thought it would be better to find a sustainable solution, such as linking these people with their local bank. However, when I went to the bank manager and explained to him what I had in mind, he was convinced that I was joking. When he realized that I was completely serious, he explained to me that banks could not lend money to the poor because they could not provide any collateral.

I did not give up and proceeded to meet with higher officials in the bank and argued with them. No luck. Finally, I offered myself as the guarantor of the loans. I was determined to show the bank officers that their fear was unfounded. I loaned money and people paid back, convincing me that loaning to the poor entailed no more risk than lending money to the rich with collateral.

Unfortunately, the bank officers remained unconvinced. Even after I demonstrated the success of the program in five districts, with excellent results, they refused to adopt it as part of their regular business. So in 1983, I decided to set up Grameen Bank as a separate bank for the poor.

Today, Grameen operates in 39,000 out of a total of 68,000 villages in Bangladesh. It lends to 2.4 million borrowers, 94% of whom are poor women. Our 97% repayment rate, which is higher than most lending institutions, confirms that loans do not need to be tied with collateral to be repaid.

Grameen is not just a traditional bank which happens to serve a poor population. To be successful, both as a poverty alleviation program and as a bank, Grameen had to do two things: reach the poorest and ensure credit discipline.

Quite frequently in the literature, one will encounter situations where "rural" and "poor" are being used interchangeably. Another common practice is to speak about the "small" or "marginal" farmer, armed with some firm belief that this is a synonym for the poor.

Instead of identifying occupations or geographic locations, the conceptually safe policy would be to define them as some bottom $x$% of the population. Grameen's target is the bottom 50% of the population below the poverty line, primarily women, as they bear the greater burden of poverty. In a Muslim country like Bangladesh, it is an almost impossible situation to attract women borrowers. Faced with the opposition from the religious leaders and frightening rumors[1] about what will happen to a woman if she takes a loan from Grameen, it is only the desperate women who finally push their way through to form the first group.

These groups gradually set the level of economic conditions for future members. The less poor stay away because they do not enjoy being classified with the destitute. In addition, all the work of Grameen is done at the doorstep of the members. Therefore, it is very difficult to conceal one's economic status from Grameen.

The second issue is that of credit discipline. Credit without strict discipline is nothing but charity. Charity does not help overcome poverty. Poverty is like being surrounded completely by high walls. Charity is a package thrown into this walled-in existence that will lighten the load for a few days. A meaningful poverty alleviation program is one that helps people gather the strength to make cracks in the walls around them.

We achieve credit discipline through our system of "social collateral." Borrowers are landless women who form groups of five to receive loans. The two poorest women receive their loans first. The other women in the

---

[1] Alan Jolis, a novelist who has co-written *Banker to the Poor: The Autobiography of Muhammad Yunus* (Aurum Press), reports that supporters of the fundamentalist party Islamic Society burned down microcredit banks, attacked borrowers, and condemned microcredit as un-Islamic because it helps women become self-employed. Jolis writes in the *International Herald Tribune*: "Every woman borrower I interviewed in Dhaka, Chittagong, and Cox's Bazaar had suffered enormously at the hands of fundamentalists. Some were beaten; others were told they would be denied proper Islamic burial; still others were told that Grameen would sell them into slavery, feed them to tigers, take them out to the sea and drown them, or tattoo their arms with a number and secretly turn them into Christians."

group do not begin receiving their loans until the first two begin regular payments. This provides a strong peer pressure/peer support network: peer pressure at times when a member willfully tries to violate Grameen's rules, and peer support at times when a member falls into any difficulty in pursuing his economic activity.

### Entrepreneurs Are a Select Group of People

In many Third World countries, the overwhelming majority of people make a living through self-employment. Because economists are unable to fit this phenomenon into their rigid framework, self-employment becomes lumped into a category called the "informal sector," something that is not seen as a desirable situation. In fact, economists argue that the sooner these countries eliminate the informal sector, the better off they will be.

What a shame! Instead of supporting the creativity of the people by creating empowering policies and institutions, we become eager to fit them into boxes that we have created. Yet the informal sector resulted from people's effort to create their own jobs. Anyone with a minimum understanding of people and society would have come forward with hope to build upon what exists and take it to higher levels, rather than pulling the rug from under it.

Reduction of poverty must be a continuous process of asset creation, so that the asset base of a poor family becomes stronger at each economic cycle, enabling them to earn, invest, and save. Poor people cannot ensure a larger share of return for their work because their initial economic base is paper-thin. Only when one can gradually build up an asset base can one command a better share for one's work.

Self-employment, supported by credit, has greater potential of improving the asset base than wage employment. In addition, the capital cost for generation of each wage-employment job is quite high. Thus, there is a strong case for self-employment based on sound economic reasons.

The most important distinction between wage and self-employment concerns the role of women. When plans are made for providing employment for the vast population, planners often think about job facilities for men only. Poor women simply do not enter the economic picture at all. And yet the skills that they attain from doing all kinds of work within the home can easily be channelled into income-generating activities. Making handicraft items, raising domestic animals, and growing fruits and vegetables—all these can open the doors to earnings for many women.

If we truly seek to help the poorest, we must serve women. Women traditionally stay home and run the family with virtually nothing to manage with. If one member of the family has to starve, there seems to be an unwritten rule that it should be the mother.

Consequently, given the opportunity to fight against hunger and poverty, a poor woman turns out to be a superior fighter compared to a poor man. Poor women have an intense drive to move up: they are hard working, concerned about their human dignity, and willing to make sacrifices for the well-being of their children.

Credit provides a woman an income-generating activity without the usual sacrifices required under a wage-employment situation. She does not have to leave her habitat and her children. She does not have to learn a new skill or adapt herself to a new job. She can do whatever she does best and earn money doing it.

At Grameen, we follow the principle that the borrower knows best. We encourage our borrowers to make their own decisions. When a nervous borrower asks a member of the Grameen staff to tell her what would be a good business idea for her, the staff member is trained to respond in the following way: "I am sorry, but I am not smart enough to give you a good business idea. Grameen has lots of money, but no business ideas. If Grameen had good business ideas also, do you think Grameen would have given the money to you? It would have used the money itself, and made more money."

Consequently, not only do women generate income, but they also become empowered in the process. The social impact of Grameen speaks for itself. I firmly believe that all human beings are potential entrepreneurs; Grameen has shown this to be true.

## Capitalism Is Reliant upon Profit Maximization

We are convinced that the capitalist economy must be fuelled only by greed. Only profit maximizers are willing to play in the marketplace and try their luck.

However, I profoundly believe, and Grameen's experience substantially affirms this point, that social goals can replace greed as a powerful motivational force. Approached methodically, enterprises driven by social consciousness can become an effective force in the marketplace.

The success of such enterprises can be seen with the Grameen companies. Grameen Phone is a nationwide cellular phone company which serves customers in the urban and rural areas of Bangladesh. Many of the Grameen borrowers become the telephone ladies of the village. They own cellular phones and sell the service of the phone to the villagers earning better incomes. Ultimately, the Grameen borrowers will own the telephone company, by buying up the shares, as occurred in the case of Grameen Bank.

Another company that Grameen has created is Grameen Cybernet. The company was started in 1996 to offer Internet access to over 2,500 customers in Dhaka. It will extend its services to the rural areas as Grameen Phone covers the villages with their telephone network. The Internet will bring the global job market to remote villages. Young people can work on jobs in data entry, Web-page design, answering services through dedicated telephones and the like without leaving their villages. Again, Grameen Cybernet will be owned by the poor.

A third company is Grameen Energy. Its purpose is to bring solar and other renewable energy sources to Bangladeshi villages, 65% of which do not have grid energy. Grameen Energy will operate by creating micro-power companies, owned, and operated by the local poor.

In conventional development strategy, power plants, telecommunications, and other forms of infrastructure are either owned by the richest in the country, or multinationals, or both and, consequently, serve their interests. Grameen and microcredit lead the way in acting in a poor-friendly way.

Lastly, we cannot solve the problem of poverty with the same theoretical framework under which we have created it. It is time we got serious about reducing poverty and searched for a new framework that would help us fulfill this responsibility. ■

The biographical sketch was drawn using the following sources:

"From Tiny Acorns." *The Economist:* December 12-18, 1998.

Smith, Emily. "Creating a Nation of Entrepreneurs—Loan by Loan." *Business Week:* August 29, 1994.

The editors of *Business Week.* "Stars of Asia." *Business Week:* June 29, 1998.

## Online Resources

- **Featured company**
  Grameen Bank
  http://www.grameen-info.org

- **Related article**
  "Microcredit No Panacea for Poor Women"
  By Nan Dawkins Scully
  Microenterprise development has helped extremely poor women survive economic crises in the short term. However, three popular misconceptions permeate the current rhetoric regarding microenterprise development and encourage its mischaracterization as a panacea.
  http://www.igc.apc.org/dgap/micro.html

- **Related Web site**
  Microcredit Summit
  In 1997, the Microcredit Summit launched a campaign to reach 100 million of the world's poorest families, especially the women of those families, with credit for self-employment by 2005. The Summit's Web site features success stories, publications and resources, best practices, and papers.
  http://www.microcreditsummit.org/

# PART 4

# TOUGH BUSINESS CHALLENGES

# Piloting a High Flier

## Cheong Choong Kong
*CEO, Singapore Airlines*
*Singapore*

"Cost consciousness has always been a hallmark of SIA manage-ment. We don't swing into a cost-cutting mode only when times get tough."

**Cheong Choong Kong**

When Asian travelers were grounded by the Asian economic crisis in 1998, few industries suffered more than the region's airlines. The likes of Taiwan's China Airlines, Garuda of Indonesia, Malaysian Airlines, and Philippine Airlines burned cash faster than jet fuel.

Not Singapore Airlines (SIA). During 1998, it expanded its holdings, built new alliances, and invested US$300 million in everything from flat TV screens and phones in economy class to gourmet menus and sleepers in first class to transform its air passenger service. The investment is paying off: SIA's sterling service makes the airline a popular choice among full-fare business travelers, who provide about 40% of its revenues.

Much of the credit goes to CEO Cheong Choong Kong, 59. *Fortune* magazine, which selected Cheong as Asia's Businessman of the Year for 1998, reports: "Tactically, Cheong shifted capacity from troubled routes within the region to thriving long-haul runs to the U.S., Europe, and Australia. Strategically, he made Singapore Airlines a stronger global player by continuing to offer service ranked by many as the best in the world."

Cheong, a former university professor, joined SIA in 1974 as an assistant manager of reservations, then worked in almost every department in the company, including personnel, marketing, and information technology. Since becoming deputy chairman and CEO in 1996, he has distinguished himself by sticking to his long-term vision for sharpening his company's international competitiveness through rigorous cost control and prudent expansion. In this speech, which Cheong delivered at the launch of SIA's product upgrade in September 1998, the savvy manager discusses how these two approaches have allowed SIA to grow while everyone else is struggling to survive.

W e have been saying that today's event is the biggest Singapore Airlines product announcement ever. When you consider how many big announcements we have made in our lifetime, including announcements of several huge aircraft orders worth tens of billions of dollars in total, you will have some idea of the scale of this product launch.

Very often, when a slick salesman waxes lyrical about the outstanding features of his product or service, he leaves the price tag to the end, after he has convinced his audience that, regardless of what it will cost them, they will want what he's selling. Well, I am no slick salesman, so I am going to break the rules and tell you the price upfront. The cost of the new product that we are unveiling today is over S$500 million.

Now you know the price, but you still don't know what we—or perhaps I should say, what our customers—are getting for our money. Our new product extends to all three classes of our Megatop 747, as well as to other aircraft types in our fleet, and also to service on the ground. It is a total product launch.

You may wonder why we are spending such a vast sum of money on launching a new product at this particular time, when East Asia is in the midst of a financial crisis, and when most airlines in the region, ourselves not excepted, are experiencing losses or have significantly reduced operating surpluses. In responding to the crisis, we must clearly distinguish between the strategic and the tactical.

The prevailing economic turbulence may last three years or even longer. We have implemented, and will continue to put in place, tactical measures to reduce the damage. Our strategies, however, are directed at the long term, and these will not change. Unlike some other carriers, we have the wherewithal to withstand the current economic onslaught and stay the course, particularly if we remain nimble and do whatever is tactically necessary to stay out of serious trouble.

We will also remain true to those core values that have served us so well all these years. One of these is total dedication to the customer. This major, expensive launch of our product and service is made in that spirit.

The commitment to this enormous program was made before the economic crisis set in. One may ask whether we would have proceeded if we knew the troubles ahead, and if we did, whether we would have done it on a more modest scale.

Let me tell you that we would have proceeded regardless. The Asian crisis affects mainly carriers based in this part of the world. SIA competes with major players all over the globe, many of which are in the pink of health. In any case, our customers expect nothing but the best from SIA, and the best is what they will get. The competitor who attempts to steal a march on us in the all-important areas of product and service does so in the knowledge that his advantage can only be temporary.

Back to the turbulent times besetting Asian carriers. We regard these problems seriously and are taking the necessary steps to protect ourselves. These include accepting a much lower growth rate than is characteristic of SIA, and being prepared even to bring that rate down to zero if necessary. We are deferring deliveries of a total of 11 aircraft over the next two years, and we are ready to increase that number if needed. We are redeploying our aircraft from the troubled Asian arena to the less tumultuous European and Australasian routes.

Cost consciousness has always been a hallmark of SIA management; we don't swing into a cost-cutting mode only when times get tough. We constantly subject our costs to scrutiny, and it is this habitual vigilance that helps us avoid radical surgery during bad times. By way of illustration, over the five-year period from 1993 to 1998, our production in terms of capacity ton-kilometers expanded 43%. During that same period, our staff numbers, if you exclude operating crew, rose a mere 2%.

A large portion of our employees are playing their part by voluntarily forgoing their wage increments this year, a touching demonstration indeed of loyalty. Despite our efforts to defend the revenue base and reduce costs, we cannot escape the effects of the crisis entirely. Times are bad, and the airline's profits will be eroded considerably, but it is highly unlikely, as of now, that it will end the financial year with a loss.

As for the long term, our objectives and strategies remain unchanged. We aim to become a global group of airlines and airline-related companies. We already have more than 25 subsidiaries in the SIA Group engaged in a variety of airline-related activities, ranging from cargo handling to security services. These companies serve not only SIA and SilkAir, but over 50 other corporate customers in Singapore alone.

We are developing these businesses not only within Singapore, but in other countries as well. If we confine ourselves to Singapore, with its trend of increasing business costs and its endemic shortage of resources, particularly human resource, we will have to resign ourselves to a steady decline of our rate of return on investment. So we go overseas, to places where there is room for much higher rates of growth and where lower cost of operations allows higher rates of return.

We also know that we cannot afford to ignore industry trends: we must expand our global reach by entering into alliances with suitable partners. Otherwise, no matter how good our product, we shall be left behind by the competition. So we entered into alliances with Ansett, Air New Zealand, and Lufthansa.

We can afford to take a long-term view because we have the means to make such investments. We probably have the strongest balance sheet of any major airline. This S$500-million launch is a demonstration of our faith in the long-term health of our industry, a promise that Singapore Airlines will stay at the forefront of airline service and product innovation. ■

The biographical sketch was drawn using the following source:
Kraar, Louis. "Asia's Businessman of the Year." *Fortune:* February 1, 1999.

# Online Resources

- **Featured company**
Singapore Airlines
http://www.singaporeair.com

- **Related articles**
"Cutting Costs without Cutting People"
By Tod Snodgrass
The way most companies deal with cost cutting is to fire people. But there are alternatives. One that's very effective, though usually ignored, is attacking discretionary overhead costs.
http://www.smartbiz.com/sbs/arts/exe126.htm

"The Cheapest CEO in America"
By Marc Ballon
Find out what the most bone-tight CEO in America has to say about frugality—and why renowned Harvard Business School professor and author John Kotter says cheap is exactly what the best low-cost operators are not. Plus, learn some tips from tightwads.
http://www.inc.com/incmagazine/archives/10970521.html

# Birthing a "Bricks and Clicks" Business

*Francis Yeoh*

*Managing Director, YTL Corporation*

*Malaysia*

"Successful leadership is about quickly responding to change. 'WWW' may stand for more than 'World Wide Web'; if you don't change to embrace it, you might be asking yourself, 'What Went Wrong?' "

**Francis Yeoh**

How do you improve on YTL Corp., one of Malaysia's largest and most profitable infrastructure companies? YTL managing director Francis Yeoh believes the answer lies in taking the company into the brave new world of e-commerce. Yeoh, who was conferred the title of Tan Sri, one of Malaysia's highest honors, took over the family-owned firm—named after his father and company founder Yeoh Tiong Lay—at age 24 and turned it into one of Malaysia's leading construction firms in ten years. YTL is now an infrastructure player with cement, property development, and hotel operations. The firm has a market capitalization of US$2.3 billion and has enjoyed over 50% compounded annual growth return for the last ten years. It is regularly cited as one of Asia's leading components in regional surveys.

The 47-year-old Yeoh attributes the company's success to what he describes as its "culture of hard work and the ability to innovate and deliver to the customer a level of service and a product that the customer wants to buy." He explains: "Our products are tailored toward consumer satisfaction. For example, we are selling the cheapest power in the world at 3.86 cents per kilowatt-hour. The cost of the Express Rail Link (which link's Malaysia's international airport to the city) is, at about US$10, the cheapest travel per kilometer in the world in a high-speed train. This principle also applies to YTL's Ritz Carlton, where the US$70 per night rate is the lowest among the Ritz Carltons in the world."

He also takes pride in YTL's "constant feedback system." Yeoh is known for holding "cabinet meetings" with his team of 30 senior managers every Monday at 10 a.m. on the dot. He claims that YTL has achieved "a balance of entrepreneurial and managerial skills."

The self-assured British-trained civil engineer believes that YTL's strengths, coupled with the power of information technology to leverage the company's competitiveness, is the key to its continued growth. YTL is one of the first Old Economy blue chip companies to transform itself to meet the challenges of the new economy. In the following article, Yeoh shares his insights on the leadership imperatives of the new economy, YTL's strategic vision, and the challenges faced by Old Economy businesses.

I have been called a visionary leader. Being visionary is not a static thing; you have to be on the ball all the time, be circumspect, and face reality.

You have to face the new realities of the new economy, which should be called the "nude" economy because the Internet makes business more transparent. Since the Internet allows information to be centrally transmitted on a network, and as content providers provide an inordinate amount of information for all and sundry on the World Wide Web, information is no longer the purview of the few. As a medium, the Internet is successful because it is an open architecture, and that is reflected in open business models that promote competition and innovation.

This means that New Economy companies are "naked" before their customers. Their CEOs must realize this fact and drive change from the top. Otherwise, they have little chance of survival in the new competitive landscape, which requires a whole new way of doing business.

Electronic commerce enables power to shift from the sellers of goods and services to consumers who are empowered to trade with suppliers offering the best deals. As supply chains are compressed, services that were once bundled to add value to the chain are being broken up. For example, in banking services, a transfer between bank accounts costs over US$1.27 if done by a teller, 27 cents if transacted over the cash machine, and one cent over the Internet. As a result, the role of intermediaries is marginalized and their survival is predicated on finding new value-added services in the supply chain.

Old Economy companies focused on increasing ROI and cost reductions and improving customer service to achieve higher efficiencies and cost-effective operations. With the advent of e-commerce, the battleground has shifted to innovation and the power of technology to improve price-to-performance ratios and broaden a company's range of products and services.

## YTL's Strategic Vision

How does YTL fit into the new competitive landscape? We have fully embraced its new realities and have launched YTL's strategic vision to transform the company from a "bricks and mortar" to a "bricks and clicks" enterprise.

As we move into the world of e-commerce, we will strive to maintain our leadership position in our core businesses. We aim to achieve this through partnerships and strategic acquisitions of e-commerce companies to create new and expanded markets through improved product offerings, faster time to market, and value-added services. These alliances will transform the way YTL conducts business by changing our interface with our customers, partners, suppliers, and employees and by enabling our company to compete in more cost-effective ways. These partnerships include:

- YTL's 20% stake in the e-Hotel Internet Portal, a business-to-business (B2B) e-procurement portal for the Malaysian hotel industry. The expected benefits to the e-Hotel Portal consortium include enhanced operating efficiency, increased brand awareness, improved synergy, better industry and market information for management and decision-making, and a platform and channel for promotions.
- YTL's 10% stake in the Malaysian Construction B2B procurement portal. The move is expected to result in efficiencies for the company's construction business.
- YTL's 50% stake in PropertyNetAsia.com. The portal will roll out a Pan-Asian property listing and be e-commerce-enabled.
- The establishment of YTL e-Solutions Sdn. Bhd. and an Internet Competency Centre. The former has an initial capital of 300 million Malaysian ringgit to acquire strategic stakes in e-commerce-related

companies in Malaysia and abroad. The latter, comprised of e-commerce experts, will forge strategic alliances with high-technology companies.

In the near future, we will roll out BintangWalk.com, a fully interactive Web site showcasing the vibrancy of the commercial area and its restaurants and eateries in the Bintang Walk precinct. The site will also feature online bookings of hotel rooms, a shopping cart offering best buys from merchants, live video images, and a virtual tour of Bintang Walk.

All these efforts will converge into building YTL's community of 500,000 loyal customers. Our company will offer premium services to this growing community to increase the "stickiness" of customer relationships. We also aim to explore cross-selling opportunities within YTL's full range of product and service offerings.

### Embrace Change or Else

The Internet is not a fad; it is here to stay. It is the greatest enabling technology in history. Any Old Economy company that ignores this technology, which is superb in its ability to communicate, run the risk of living in Jurassic Park.

I would recommend that Old Economy companies look into the Internet and service their customers as well as they could. Now, because customers are expecting a high level of service and at a lower price, I don't think Old Economy companies can afford to ignore the Internet. Five years from now, e-commerce will be so pervasive that it will become a way of life. Old Economy companies should not bury their heads in the sand with the advent of e-commerce.

Which companies will survive in the new economy? I would bet on companies that have been around for a long time—the GEs of the world, the ones with big market shares in the old economy but are not stubborn or arrogant enough to ignore e-commerce. Any company that has a big market share in Old Economy businesses will stop growing by not investing in e-commerce.

Take British company Virgin, for example. The company launched a service enabling customers to buy cars from Europe and have them delivered to their homes. Such service effectively prevents them from paying 5,000 to 6,000 pounds more per car than in the rest of Europe—an anomaly in the British car market. Virgin founder Richard Branson's innovative service wipes out the middleman in the supply chain.

Many successful companies become complacent until the Richard Bransons—people who are innovative about customer service—shake up the industry. And Branson wins because he understands what his customers want, and he delivers. Today, Virgin Airlines fetches you in a helicopter if you are within 50 kilometers of the airport and gives you a massage while you are on board the plane.

Successful leadership is about quickly responding to change. "WWW" may stand for more than "World Wide Web"; if you don't change to embrace it, you might be asking yourself, "What Went Wrong?" I don't want to have that post-mortem when it's too late. ■

---

This article is written from extracts of Long Shih Rome's interviews with Tan Sri Dato' Francis Yeoh as well as articles in *Smart Investor*, a leading financial magazine in Malaysia. Long is the editor of *Smart Investor*.

## Online Resources

- **Featured company**
  YTL Corporation Bhd.
  http://www.ytl.com.my

- **Related article**
  "Do Bricks Float?"
  By David Matthew
  Three techniques to reinvent your company for the Internet economy
  http://www.cio.com/archive/101500_hs_bricks.html

- **Related Web site**
  The E-Business Research Center
  By the editors of *CIO* magazine
  From small business to multinational, electronic commerce will change the way you do business. This research center examines the current state and future directions of conducting commerce on the Net. http://www.cio.com/forums/ec/

# Chinese Family Values in Transition

*David K. P. Li*

Chairman and CEO, Bank of East Asia Ltd.

*Hong Kong SAR*


"Today's need for financial accountability, to attract outside investment and satisfy modern accounting standards, is forcing the traditional-style Chinese companies to change the way they conduct business."

**David K. P. Li**


David K. P. Li, one of Hong Kong's most respected businessmen, is the chairman and chief executive officer of the Bank of East Asia Ltd. Li joined the bank in 1969, and was named chief executive in 1986 and chairman in 1995.

Li, born in Britain of a wealthy family, studied mathematics at London University until, according to one published report, he realized that somebody in his class was better than him. Switching to law at Cambridge, he still became an accountant because he was not satisfied with taking second place in his final law exams. Despite having led a life of privilege, Li has been quoted as having but one wish—that the day held 12 hours more so that he could get more work done.

In addition to sitting on a number of boards of public companies, Li is a member of the Exchange Fund Advisory Committee, Banking Advisory Committee, and the Hong Kong Association of Banks, all of which play a significant role in shaping Hong Kong's monetary policy. His directorships include Campbell Soup Co., Dow Jones, Hongkong Telecom, San Miguel Brewery, Sime Darby, and Vitasoy International.

Li is known to have *guanxi*—literally, "relationships," or influence—in China, where personal relationships usually make the difference between success and failure. He has assembled many cooperative ventures with partners from both the West and the mainland. In the following article, Li explores the Chinese business enterprise and management style, describes how they are changing, and predicts the dynamic development of Greater China.

T he financial turmoil that has rocked East Asian equity and currency markets is a painful, but necessary, reminder that the Asian way of business is not immune to the unforgiving logic of global markets. In retrospect, perhaps some had become too complacent in the seemingly unlimited success of the region. Instead of paying attention to financial fundamentals, there were lectures about the superiority of so-called "Asian values."

Asian values, to some, seemed to be a carte blanche for fiscal hubris. In short, some became greedy. Business fundamentals were ignored in pursuit of short-term profit. Despite all this, it is important to remember that the core values that shaped the Asian miracle have not changed. The remarkable work ethic of Asian workers, a disciplined commitment to save, a commitment to education, and support for governments that remain strongly pro-business are still, and will continue to be, the key reasons for the past and future success of Asian economies.

When people talk about Asian values, they are often talking about the Confucian principles that guide the "Chinese business enterprise"—one of the fundamental business units in Asia and a key client base for the Bank of East Asia since it was founded in 1918. Outside Japan, Chinese family-owned businesses control a large proportion of Asia's economic assets.

There is no doubt that the market crash highlighted some of the weaknesses in the way Asian enterprises conduct business. What may surprise many, though, will be the speed of the recovery. The history of this region (and of the overseas Chinese, or "global Chinese entrepreneurial network") is one of adaptation and change in the face of uncertainty and hostility.

Let me be so bold as to argue that the next century is still going to be the Pacific century. As any good Chinese entrepreneur knows, uncertainty and opportunity go together.

As we enter the twenty-first century, the environment that produced the Chinese enterprise is vanishing. Armed with the latest technologies and practices, Japanese and Western management executives are providing fiercer competition. Global market forces are pushing so-called family enterprises to operate in a more open management style. The companies and economies that will flourish into the next century are those that can best adapt to ever-changing social and technological environments. Chinese enterprises are no different.

## Networks of Relationships

Just what is a "Chinese enterprise"? It is both your favorite Chinese restaurant and some of the largest financial and business enterprises in the world. Traditionally, the Chinese enterprise began as a trading or retailing concern in a city like Hong Kong, Taipei, Jakarta, Singapore, Bangkok, Manila, or Saigon.

Through its network of relationships, it could do business with counterparts throughout East Asia. These networks extended to the villages in Fujian and Guangdong provinces in China that produced most of the original immigrants to East Asia. Members of these same families forged international networks.

Over the years, many of the more ambitious enterprises have become major international conglomerates in industries such as property, shipping, manufacturing, retailing, distribution, and telecommunications. Their operations may be in Southeast Asia, Europe, or North America. Most of all, today, they are providing the overwhelming majority of offshore investment in mainland China—the ultimate marketplace and their ancestral home.

It is not surprising that this success has aroused interest in the Chinese management style. I am delighted that the university I attended, Cambridge, now has a professor of Chinese management. This interest has been aroused for a very simple reason: Western academics and managers think that the traditional Chinese family enterprise can teach Western companies how to work better.

Perhaps the key difference between Western and Chinese enterprises is the importance of families and the relationships they use to grow their businesses. The Chinese enterprise is typically owned by the family, and is managed by the family under the hierarchical regiment of one man—

the patriarch. He is the board of directors and executive committee rolled into one. Where the Japanese company has to achieve consensus and the Western company needs to do market and other research, the Chinese company relies on just one person's seasoned instinct and acumen.

## Pure Opportunism

Overseas Chinese traditionally relied on secrecy and hidden networks to survive in hostile and uncertain environments. The company's patriarch was traditionally part of a larger web of business relationships where "who you know" matters most. These relationships complement strategy, research, and contracts: The tallest building in Hong Kong, Central Plaza, for example, was half-built before the main contract was signed.

This way of doing business has provided an important competitive advantage for the Chinese enterprise. It has allowed, and still allows, the Chinese to run extremely flexible organizations. One respected person makes the decisions, so the company is swift on its feet. It is a structure that lends itself to pure opportunism.

I know of no other type of organization that can move as swiftly and effectively. The fast decision-making process enables traditional Chinese family firms to react quickly to threats as well as opportunities.

Today's need for financial accountability, to attract outside investment, and satisfy modern accounting standards, is forcing the traditional-style Chinese companies to change the way they conduct business. This is true not only with corporate governance but also with matters such as personnel policy.

Today, I am the chairman and chief executive of the Bank of East Asia, but I am the only family member in the 4,000-strong organization. Our managers are recruited and promoted on the basis of their ability. We have an open management where creative thinking is encouraged. As a result, we are competitive. Indeed, we could have never grown into the largest local bank in Hong Kong without standard Western management practices.

A new generation of Chinese executives is armed with MBAs from the finest business schools in the world. They understand that "what you know" is as important as "who you know." They have created a new set of relationships, encompassing not only family but also their former classmates and their new business associates. The new generation is eager to exploit new technologies, happy to hire specialists and professional managers, and prepared to go to the stock market to raise funds.

What does all this mean for Hong Kong and China? Despite the financial turmoil, I have never been more bullish about the future prospects of Greater China and the Asian economies. The single most important economic development of the next century will be the integration of China's economy with the global trading system. The key to this success will be partnering with global Chinese entrepreneurs.

The overseas Chinese were the first to recognize the economic potential that China was creating through reform. Hong Kong, the eighth largest trading entity in the world, remains not only China's chief gateway to and from the world, but an example of Chinese economic success. Within ten years, we will witness the consolidation of China's economic potential. By then, China will be well on its way to establishing a legal system, and new infrastructure will have changed the face of China.

As China continues to evolve, you will see hotbeds for economic growth with similar patterns of success as those experienced by companies in places like California's Silicon Valley. Over the past five years, China has spent billions of dollars updating its information infrastructure. Underlying China's technological potential is a large corps of first-rate scientific talent. As China moves ahead, developing everything from rocketry to biotechnology to lasers and optics, it will become a twenty-first century scientific superpower. Indeed, China is the only emerging industrial economy that is likely to challenge the United States, Japan, or Europe on the frontiers of technology.

This has awesome implications for Chinese entrepreneurs. The combination of China's scientific potential, Taiwan's expertise in production engineering, and Hong Kong's ability to finance, package, and market products will open the way for the dynamic development of Greater China.

Over the next 50 years, China will also develop an immense and complex consumer society with more than a billion eager consumers. We already are seeing the emergence of new Chinese companies creating products and services for the Chinese market, such as Chinese MTV. In time, Chinese brands will go global and Chinese culture, like U.S. culture, will become an important export and global force.

China's new consumer culture will be made possible by the single most important economic development of the last half of this century—the opening of the Chinese economy by Chinese entrepreneurs and their foreign partners. It will have enormous implications for global prosperity and stability. With patience, and with understanding, the integration of the Chinese system into the world economy will herald the beginning of a new era of global economic vibrancy.

At this time of uncertainty, this new era may seem rather distant. Integration requires the building of genuine understanding—on both sides. The way forward, though, is through partnership—partnership between Western, overseas Chinese, and mainland Chinese companies. It will be a partnership of different management systems built on relationships and trust. Both sides must be willing to respect each other and learn from each other.

Although it will be a slow process, these successful partnerships will learn and change each other. In the end, the question of "Chinese" and "Western" styles will gradually fade and only two styles of management will pervade: "good" and "bad." ■

---

This article first appeared in **Outlook**, which is published by Andersen Consulting (www.ac.com). Reprinted by permission.

The biographical sketch was drawn using the following sources:

Kohut, John. "The Boom Merchants." *Asia Inc.*: February 1997.

Kraar, Louis. "Meet 25 People You Ought to Know." *Fortune*: December 13, 1989.

## Online Resources

• **Featured company**
Bank of East Asia
http://www.hkbea.com/whp_welcome/whp_welmain.html

• **Related articles**
"Asian Values Revisited"
From *The Economist*
Asian values did not explain the tigers' astonishing economic successes, and they do not explain their astonishing economic failures.
http://www.economist.com/editorial/freeforall/library/index_special_collection.html

"The Bamboo Network: Asia's Family-Run Conglomerates"
By Murray Weidenbaum
Why have family-owned conglomerates founded by ethnic Chinese become key economic factors throughout Asia? The answers are trust and tradition.
http://www.strategy-business.com/policy/98106/index.html

# Coping in the
# Complex China Market

*Edward Tse*

*Former Managing Partner for Greater China*
*Booz-Allen & Hamilton*
*Hong Kong SAR*

"Now that many multinational companies have completed their market
entry into China, the major challenge is how to grow their businesses
profitably."

**Edward Tse**

Edward Tse, the executive vice-president for corporate planning and
development at Cable & Wireless KHT Ltd., is the former managing partner of
Booz-Allen & Hamilton's Greater China operations. At his former position,
Tse, who holds a B.S. and an M.S. from the Massachusetts Institute of
Technology as well as an M.B.A. and a Ph.D. from the University of California,
Berkeley, provided consultancy advice to multinational companies and Chinese
enterprises on strategy, operations, and organization.

In this article, he writes how, for too long, investors in China have taken an
overly simplistic approach to doing business. Companies must understand
diversity and complexity if they are to meet the demanding challenge of
profitable growth.

Procter & Gamble sells in more than 500 cities in China.
Nestlé has a dominant position in the coffee market.
Motorola has built a strong brand image. China is already one of
the largest markets for Ericsson and Nokia.

Many multinational companies (MNCs) have completed their market
entry into China. Now they face the major challenge of how to grow their
businesses profitably. The factors involved—customers, markets,
products, competition, sales and distribution channels, organization, and
human resources—are all changing.

Following are some pointers for coping in a rapidly changing operating environment.

## Understand the Regulations Affecting Your Industry

Regulation has a great impact on the competitive dynamics and degree of freedom for companies operating in China. It can be measured by two dimensions: product market approach and ownership approach.

The product market approach applies to companies' product offerings and market activities. Typical attributes include what product companies are allowed to make and sell; what controls exist on pricing; and how the goods can be distributed.

The ownership approach refers to the ownership type and structure that companies utilize to set up subsidiaries in China. Depending on the industry, various ownership approaches—such as wholly foreign-owned enterprises and cooperative joint ventures—are made available to foreign companies.

China's regulatory context also varies over time. For example, when China opened its carbonated drink business in the 1980s, foreign companies such as Coca-Cola and PepsiCo were not allowed to hold majority equity positions in their joint ventures. The government assigned joint venture partners and controlled the number of joint ventures. Today, foreign carbonated drink companies can have majority ownership in their joint ventures up to a certain limit, and they can choose their own joint venture partners.

## Be Aware of Market Dynamics

Initially, MNCs held a simplistic view of the Chinese market. Companies in the consumer products industry, for example, believed in the logic that "if there are 1.2 billion Chinese, and if each person buys $x$ number of products per year, then our market in China will be $y$."

However, the needs and characteristics of various market segments differ greatly. There is enormous diversity among major urban centers such as Beijing, Shanghai, and Guangzhou, as well as among large cities, small cities, and rural areas within the same geographic region. For example, the official household income level of the top three urban centers is seven times greater than that of surrounding rural areas.

In addition, the cost of servicing the market and the nature of competition often varies by market segment. As a result, the real market size can be very different from that originally anticipated. Some companies have moved away from this broad-brush approach, focusing instead on a few markets.

Another mistake that MNCs often make is to focus only on existing consumer demand. In an emerging market like China, however, policy, regulations, income, and consumption patterns can change rapidly. Companies that anticipate these changes can turn them to their advantage.

Ting Hsin anticipated the need for more convenient and hygienic fast food and was the first to offer instant noodles packaged in a bowl. This package format became very popular, and Ting Hsin has captured more than a 30% share of the instant noodle market in China.

## Focus on Operational Efficiencies

Today, many MNCs tend to focus their efforts on marketing and distribution. But, in doing so, they often neglect the important operational aspects of their businesses. When MNCs first entered China, many thought local costs were low and therefore did not pay attention to managing efficient operations. However, the actual costs of doing business in China can be high. Local labor and management costs are increasing rapidly, and expatriate costs are often higher than expected.

Manufacturing and sourcing costs can also be steep. The comparatively low labor productivity, inadequate inventory management skills and systems, and sub-optimal quality control contribute to high operating costs.

As a result, many MNCs in China find that while they are selling in an emerging market, their costs can be the same as in the industrialized world. In one fast-moving consumer goods joint venture, the unit manufacturing cost in China was, at best, at parity with other plants around the world. For some products, it was more than 30% higher.

## Build a Strong Local Organization

Successful companies in China are the ones that build strong local organizations. Managers in China need to be entrepreneurial, willing to accept ambiguities, sensitive to local business culture, and have a nose for capturing broad trends. They also need to maintain effective communications with the rest of the company, especially headquarters, to set the right level of expectation for their China operation and to communicate the challenges of doing business in the country.

Some well-performing MNCs have found that while localization is the right long-term goal, complete localization in China will remain difficult for the next three to five years given the imbalance in the supply and demand of qualified local managers. Companies should take a dual approach to building a local organization.

At the entry and middle management levels, company managers should make the building of a local team a top management priority. More local talent with the right basic qualities is emerging in China. Companies should identify and recruit this pool of workers, as well as equip them with the right skills.

Complete turnover of the senior management to a local team is too premature for most companies. Some companies have found that creating a core team of local and expatriate managers to share the responsibilities of communications, building the local organization, and understanding the local market and competitive environment is better.

## Find a Way to Quickly Capture and Use Market Data

Developing superior insights into the consumer, while critical in any consumer market, is particularly important in China. While there is substantial volatility in the market, there is also considerable potential to build brands and market access.

Companies should capture consumer information as a core capability within their Chinese organizations. Procter & Gamble, for example, captures Chinese consumer information using a 30-plus market research team. Traditional research approaches such as focus groups and surveys work well.

Because of the fast pace of change in China, speed in collecting information is critical. Companies must quickly focus on the fundamentals and get enough data to make business decisions. ■

## Online Resources

- **Featured companies**
  Booz-Allen & Hamilton
  http://www.bah.com

  Motorola, Inc.
  http://www.mot.com

  Nestlé S.A.
  http://www.nestle.com

  The Procter & Gamble Company
  http://www.pg.com

- **Related Web Site**
  The China Business Review
  The China Business Review, the official magazine of the US-China Business Council, features articles on topics including strategies for penetrating the Chinese market, opportunities in specific sectors, and legal developments in China's trade and investment arenas.
  http://www.chinabusinessreview.com/

  "Gold from Noodles"
  By James Hexter, Javier Perez, and Anthony Perkins
  Can you make money in China's packaged food market? There are many recipes for disaster. Three lessons: price for high affordability, rush for scale, and invest in people, not assets.
  http://mckinseyquarterly.com/countrie/gono98.asp

# Managing a Truly International Bank: The HSBC Approach to Globalization

*John Bond*

Group Chairman, HSBC Holdings Plc
United Kingdom

"Banking is 90% action and 10% strategy."

**John Bond**

Technology has played a role in the success of HSBC Holdings Plc. HSBC was the first institution to offer online banking in Britain. Last year, the company spent US$2 billion on money-saving technology, including a project to create a massive interface so customers can directly tap into its accounting systems and do their banking by any means they choose: phones, digital TV, PC, Web, or handheld devices.

Beyond HSBC's use of technology, however, is something more fundamental to the company: thrift. Chairman John Bond is known to set an example for frugality. The reserved and disciplined executive turns out the lights when he leaves a room because, "it costs US$700,000 a year just to light our ten main buildings in London." He flies economy and takes the subway to work. And his US$1.1-million total compensation in 1999 was a far cry from rural Citigroup co-chief Sanford Weill's US$164 million compensation package.

The 60-year-old Bond, who joined HSBC when he was 19 years old, after working on a cargo ship that sailed from California to Hong Kong, has certainly been witness to the growth of the international colossus. HSBC has come a long way from the 1865-founded colonial bank headquartered in Hong Kong to one of the largest banking and financial services organizations in the world. Today, it has an international network comprised of more than 5,000 offices in 80 countries and territories, servicing 23 million customers around the globe and operating in the Asia-Pacific region, Europe, the Americas, the Middle East, and Africa.

HSBC is not just huge; it's also the most efficient of the world's top banks. In 1999, every dollar of income HSBC brought in cost it 54 cents, putting it well ahead of Citigroup, at 68 cents. In the same year it reported US$6 billion in net income. Its 20.8% five-year return on equity beats not only the other majors but also international competitors like Barclays (20.2%) and ABN-Amro (17.8%).

In this article, Bond discusses the foundations of HSBC's success.

I f globalization is so ubiquitous, why is it spelled differently depending on where you come from? We hear so much about it that I'm sure many people have come to think that every significant company in every major industry is hell-bent on foreign expansion. That is just not the case.

Many businesses are international; almost none span the entire globe. With more than 220 countries on our planet, and very few businesses with a presence in more than a handful, the word "globalization" may be a misnomer. HSBC may be one of those few. HSBC Bank International Limited, our telephone banking service for expatriates, serves customers in over 190 countries. That compares to 185 countries belonging to the United Nations.

Globalization is a convenient, if ugly, shorthand for a series of complex interacting factors. One commentator recently defined globalization as the integration of finance, markets, nation-states, and technologies to a degree never witnessed before—in a way that is enabling individuals, corporations, and nation-states to reach further, faster, deeper, and cheaper than ever before.

Globalization means different things at different times to different people. To a banker, the emphasis may be on the international movement of capital; for en educator it may be about long-distance learning through new delivery channels; for governments it may be about challenges to national sovereignty. The one thing almost every commentator does agree on is that globalization is here to stay. Whatever globalization consists of, we can expect more of it.

The conventional wisdom about the internationalization of financial services ignores the fact that for many years banks have backed away from foreign ventures, the latest large-scale retreat having occurred in Southeast Asia. Historically, many of the investments made by British,

Continental, and Japanese banks to penetrate the highly competitive U.S. market, for example, have ended in ignominious retreat. The reason for these misadventures (often destroyers of shareholder value) has nearly always been the same: a failure of the entrants to a national or regional market to achieve a viable domestic base of business within a reasonable time. They didn't appreciate the exciting risk/reward ratios of their geographic extensions of domain.

HSBC is very much aware of these risks. Our group has endured as an international entity for over 130 years, while increasing shareholder value more than 20% annually, compounded over the last 30 years.

From birth, HSBC was international. It was founded in 1865 in Hong Kong, then a backwater far from the orbit of world money centers, by Scots, along with Parsees, Norwegians, Germans, and Americans on its board. Its initial territorial expansion followed trade routes to the north, south, and west. In the course of our history, we have survived some pretty turbulent times. However, we have endured to create a network of more than 5,000 offices in 80 countries and territories.

This background, which has shaped our character, is very different from that of most other major banks on the world scene, such as Citigroup or Deutsche Bank. Much more typical of international banks is that they have sallied forth in the last few decades from very powerful domestic bases.

## A Strong Balance Sheet, an Eye for Opportunity

The key to our success has been something not as fashionable today as it once was, and that is a strong balance sheet. In discussions on globalization, rarely does one hear people speak of the importance of a conservative financial position. Yet because we were founded on Scottish banking principles and because of our history, we have been unswerving in this regard and today operate with considerably less leverage than most of our major competitors. We lend about 50% of one of the most conservative balance sheets in our industry, while some of our rivals lend as much as 75% of theirs.

Without a conservative balance sheet, a bank cannot long endure the choppy seas of the world's financial oceans. Viewed in long-term perspective, international finance has grown enormously, despite occasional cyclical declines in regional or banking markets that can temporarily affect the market capitalization of high-quality institutions. This is when we step in and make strategic acquisitions, preferably without paying premium prices.

Because we have an eye for opportunity when turbulence provides it, we have prospered at a time when others are weak or struggling. At such times, our financial conservatism attracts deposits away from less sound institutions, and we look for acquisition opportunities. When the market is buffeting our competitors, then is the time to be bold. In 1965 we bought Hang Seng Bank in Hong Kong when it was experiencing a difficult period; similarly Marine Midland in the United States in 1980 and the Midland Bank in 1992 when they were facing problems. In 1997 we purchased Banco Bamerindus in Brazil, one of the largest banks in the country, again at a time when it was experiencing serious difficulties.

Our acquisitions were not merely opportunistic. In each case our decision was based on the belief that here was a good consumer franchise that we could nurture. Where there is a sound fit with our business, we are not afraid to look at good banks.

We use our selective acquisition strategy to grow because of the significant costs of building franchises de novo. It would be impossible today to create the client-based branch infrastructure of a Midland Bank: The effort would run out of money many years before a profit was in sight.

We constantly screen acquisition possibilities. Our strategic proclivities are well known to the investment banks, yet they frequently try to interest us in acquisitions where we simply fail to see value. We have been besieged with propositions to buy this or that bank in the United States or Europe, typically at large multiples. If we did buy these offerings, it would be a ridiculously expensive way to acquire share in overbanked markets, where the only way to expand client base is at the expense of a competitor.

Contrast this with the situation in an emerging market, such as Brazil, where it is possible to buy a franchise at below net asset value. This is a country where only about a quarter of the population has a bank account, so the prospects for organic growth are excellent. There is also a very favorable pricing there: Middle-class Brazilians are pleased to have a bank account and pay US$10 a month for one. There is no way you can get someone in the United Kingdom or United States to pay that.

One of the prime advantages of our international reach and scope is that the economic impact of our strategies has a ripple effect across the globe. For example, major new product development efforts can readily be migrated across borders and their costs amortized over a larger base than most of our competitors command. What's more, there is a benefit to operating in countries with varying stages of maturity in banking services. Knowhow developed in one place can be exported to another. First Direct, our pioneering U.K. telephone banking operation, contributed significantly to later HSBC telephone banking initiatives in the United States and Asia.

If franchise creation in banking is difficult, so too is product innovation. Ours is a very transparent industry with a high degree of homogeneity. If you design a brand-new banking product that's a roaring success, you might gain a lead-time of six months before somebody copies it. If you come up with an internal process innovation, the lead might be as long as 18 months before someone on your staff quits, goes to another bank, and introduces the innovation there. The lasting competitive strength in financial services is having a performance- and action-oriented corporate character, or culture, as some like to call it.

Our financial results have justified our strategy. We are one of the largest financial services organizations in the world and one of the most geographically diversified—a constant source of strength. In 1998, for instance, HSBC suffered the consequences of the Asian financial crisis, which required the largest provisions in our history. Yet in spite of these adverse conditions, we managed to produce a return on shareholders' funds of 15.5% and pay a dividend up 11% from 1997. In our view, this vindicates our strategy of geographic diversificatio, and the consequent diversity of risk.

## Tried-and-True Teamwork

Banking is not rocket science. The underlying principles of success are simple. They are (1) focus on clients, (2) good credit quality (so that your loan loss experience is better than the competitors'), and (3) tight control over expenses.

Banking is about doing: It is 90% action and 10% strategy. Tried-and-true teamwork is essential to running an international business, which, by definition, has more complexity than a domestic one. That is the key to competitive advantage. One of our outstanding characteristics is good teamwork and coordination. We have tremendous talent but, deliberately, very few management stars on the payroll.

Half of our profit is made while I sleep. So I had better know that there are people on the other side of the world who are doing things the HSBC way. If we are to provide our shareholders with something more than a portfolio of banks, there cannot be a loose federation or a do-as-you-please holding company philosophy. We are constantly working to extract cross-border benefit, thereby making the whole worth more than a sum of its parts.

One keystone of our teamwork is that we try to give people lifetime careers, which, I recognize, may be a little old-fashioned these days. But we've found no better basis for team building. As quid pro quo for job security, we pay our middle and senior executives sensibly but not excessively, meanwhile offering them a climate of fair reward, a progressive and varied career, and a good pension. Little wonder that there is a canard that HSBC stands for "Home of Scottish Bank Clerks." Jokes aside, the key to good teamwork is a stable and predictable work environment. We are not, however, reluctant to reach for new blood and recruit on the outside.

## Expense Discipline: A Matter of Culture

To succeed in the international arena, a company must have competitive fitness across all business functions. We are fanatics about expense discipline: Not only is it good for shareholders, but it permits us to tolerate price wars wherever they may flare up. I'm not bashful about telling people that I know exactly the amount of the electric bill for our headquarters building. When I leave my office, no matter how briefly, I turn off the lights. Since the onset of the Asian financial crisis we have twice tightened the rules for first-class eligibility on our executives' flights abroad. In New York our people don't stay at five-star hotels, they go to middle-range ones in downtown Manhattan.

So ingrained is this character trait that we make heroes of people who think up expense reduction ideas. The bottom-line benefits are considerable. A U.K. competitor, which is smaller and predominantly domestic, spends twice as much on travel and entertainment as we do, even though we are operating on every continent. Our total operating cost as a ratio of revenues is probably the lowest of any large international bank.

Accordingly, we are prepared for the huge productivity war brewing in banking. Every advance in information and communications technology and in financial deregulation puts pressure on our revenues by reducing customers' float. Ultimately, success will belong to the lowest-cost producer.

We have obtained fantastic productivity from our homegrown I.T. system. Unlike many banks, we do not buy core I.T. systems from external providers and we outsource as little as possible. We preserve our systems independence because we believe that it attracts the best people into our I.T. area—those who like pioneering and original work, not the frustrating game of tying together acquired software package.

As an international bank we have the ability to exploit the comparative advantage of different locations for I.T. development. We operate four software and systems development centers: in Vancouver, Buffalo, Sheffield, and Hong Kong SAR. Because of our overall control of I.T. architectures and applications, there is an unusual uniformity of systems throughout the bank; the same screens are available everywhere in the world where we operate a terminal (excepting recent acquisitions, which still have some of their legacy systems).

## Rebranding on a Global Basis

A bank so steeped in history stands in some danger of being a little complacent. But we're not backward looking. When the situation calls for it, we deviate from past patterns and can be creative in our strategies and tactics. A case in point is the global rebranding exercise launched in late 1998 and executed through 1999. All our wholly owned commercial banking subsidiaries now carry the HSBC name along with our red and white hexagon logo.

Why the change? A consistent acquirer inevitably ends up with a tapestry of regional and national brands of varying effectiveness. A few years back we operated under about 300 different names scattered around the globe. Recent structural changes in the banking market made us question the multilocal approach to branding. Merely local brands no longer have the old magic, especially in developed countries.

Symbols and artifacts with a pan-global cachet have become very powerful, from foodstuffs to high fashion wear. When we analyzed the chief drivers of value within our franchises, it turned out that a very large part of our retail profits is generated by a comparatively small segment of customers. To paraphrase Pareto's law, 20% of our customers yielded some 80% of the bottom line. Moreover, that 20% contained customers who are now highly international and geographically mobile.

Our bank managers in the developed world repeatedly found customers returning from foreign journeys complaining that we didn't have local service when we actually did, albeit disguised by another name. The opportunity to satisfy that customer, and to cement loyalty, was being lost. Among institutional customers in trade finance and wholesale and investment banking, there was a similar story: When making customer contacts, these people wasted time explaining to clients the details of our global network and its complex of names.

People get attached to names and symbols. Midland Bank was a fixture on thousands of U.K. High Streets; the same was true for Marine Midland in the upstate region of New York state. But venerability and/or familiarity should not be confused with brand strength. Our research in the United Kingdom showed that First Direct, our telephone bank, actually had a stronger brand than its Midland parent did. First Direct is 10 years old and Midland's name goes back to 1836.

This is worth pondering: In less than a decade we created a brand with greater perceived value than a name that has been around for more than 150 years. The message is clear: Customers are discerning about the sources of value. They think pragmatically. "What have you done for me lately?" is critical.

It is our aim that the HSBC brand express differentiation in the depth and quality of our services. In tune with our character, this branding exercise is being done on a very low cost basis. As the *Economist* dryly reported, "HSBC has eschewed the services of expensive image consultants. It is spending a mere US$50 million, and whatever it can filch from local banks' marketing budgets, on launching its new name—barely enough for new notepaper—to alert 30 million customers to the change." (The US$50 million excludes advertising.)

Global branding is in its infancy in the commercial banking field. Ten and 20 years hence it will be as common as in automobiles today. The institutions boasting dominant brands then will be those that caught the brand-making wave early and that offer the four Ss— service, scale, scope, and synergy. Although the day is a long way off, I think that the leading brands will be able to charge slightly higher prices because of their power to represent value to the customer.

To sum up, the foundations of our success at HSBC are a strong balance sheet, good expense control, a team culture, and the beginnings of a great global brand. We are aware of the perils and opportunities of operating internationally. Globalization is perhaps the last great frontier for business, but frontier life, remember, is exacting and exciting. ■

---

The biographical sketch was drawn using the following sources:

Capell, Kerry and Clifford, Mark. "John Bond's HSBC." *Business Week*: September 20, 1999.

Morais, Richard C. "Bullterrier Banking." *Forbes*: July 24, 2000.

## Online resources

- **Featured company**
  HSBC Holdings Plc.
  http://www.hsbc.com

- **Related articles**
  "Globalization: What Lies Ahead for Financial Services"
  By Trevor Gruzin and Robert Davidow
  Globalization in financial services has been under way since the 1980s. What lies ahead, both for companies that have made the global move and those that have not?
  http://www.ac.com/ideas/Outlook/pov/pov_globilization.html

  "Good News—It's a Small World"
  By Keith H. Hammonds
  Who cares where our cars, computers, or clothes are made? If December's "Battle of Seattle" is any indication, lots of people do. A book by two savvy journalists makes the case for globalization.
  http://www.fastcompany.com/online/34/bookreport.html

# Ba ("Shared Space"): A Place for Managing Knowledge

*Yotaro Kobayashi*

*Chairman and CEO, Fuji Xerox Co., Ltd.*
*Japan*

"Creativity is organic, and it flourishes in an intellectual ecosystem. If we turn that ecosystem into a hothouse for rapid growth, we will almost certainly damage what we are trying to produce."

**Yotaro Kobayashi**

Yotaro Kobayashi is considered a successor to Akio Morita as Japan's most prominent international industrialist. As an expert on both American and Japanese business cultures, he has gained notoriety helped redefine business leadership in today's changing global economy.

The 68-year-old Kobayashi is known for his focus on innovative management. In 1999, he received the Deming Prize for Individuals from the Japanese Union of Scientists and Engineers. The prestigious award is given to individuals who have contributed to the development of Total Quality Control (TQC) activities. Kobayashi is credited for implementing operational innovation through TQC when he was Fuji Xerox Co. Ltd.'s president, as well as for promoting its application across Xerox's global operations. He is also recognized for initiating revolutionary management methods such as the establishment of internal venture firms and a personnel management system, which includes volunteer activities outside the company as part of an employee's performance evaluation.

As chairman of the board of Fuji Xerox, Kobayashi heads a 50-50 joint venture between Fuji Photo Film and Rank Xerox (now Xerox Limited), which produces and supplies various kinds of office equipment, including color copiers, networked systems, and integrated printing systems. In this article, he describes how a corporate culture that encourages knowledge sharing is the best way to optimize a company's intellectual assets to benefit both a company and its customers.

Today, capital and labor alone are inadequate competitive weapons. Success in the international marketplace comes increasingly from giving employees the tools to express their creativity, to interact with others, and to draw upon the collective wisdom of the organization to develop unique products and services.

This process is what we mean by *knowledge management* at Fuji Xerox. The term is common, but I think our view of it is unique. Our version of knowledge management rests on a simple foundation. I am a strong believer in the virtue of patience—allowing ideas, and the products they might become, to develop at their own pace. While it is possible to force an idea along its natural evolutionary path, something is likely to be lost in the effort.

Creativity is organic, and it flourishes in an intellectual ecosystem. If we turn that ecosystem into a hothouse for rapid growth, we will almost certainly damage what we are trying to produce.

I know that many companies take a hard-line approach to knowledge management, in the conviction that only "relevant" knowledge deserves attention and resources. Yet what is irrelevant today may be of critical importance tomorrow. Ideas that are vague and ill defined right now may harbor in their shadows the revolutionary product of the future.

I suspect that few CEOs today would regard ancient Greek philosophy as knowledge relevant to their business. Joe Wilson, known as the father of Xerox and an important mentor of mine, advised me many years ago to enroll in The Aspen Institute's Executive Seminar. I did so and found that the reading list at Aspen was heavily weighted toward the classics, including Plato and Aristotle.

Did the knowledge I gained lead to a new research breakthrough in reproduction science? No. Did the ancient quest for knowledge through dialogue influence my approach to business and the management of Fuji Xerox? Absolutely!

**Explicit and Tacit Knowledge**

Knowledge management begins with definitions of terms, which inform how the company approaches tasks and goals, even how we speak. Professor Ikujiro Nonaka, one of knowledge management's influential scholars, has drawn the distinction between *explicit* and *tacit* knowledge. Explicit knowledge is the clearly defined, scientific research and information that informs much of our day-to-day business. Tacit knowledge is largely intangible and harder to define. It is knowhow, experience, personal insights, and beliefs.

I think that many companies, including Fuji Xerox, have successfully harnessed explicit knowledge, but hierarchies, bureaucracies, and cultures make it much more difficult to share tacit knowledge. My personal vision is to go beyond explicit knowledge and share our employees' personal, tacit knowledge with the rest of the organization. Ultimately, I want to create a knowledge-driven company, in both structural and human terms.

Our corporate mission statement recognizes these categories with its use of the Japanese term for knowledge, *Chi*. *Chi* implies strong overtones of tacit knowledge; it implies knowledge that has yet to be made specific or assume the form of information. The term suggests something close to wisdom, more difficult to grasp than data, strongly informed by human relationships and experience.

Our commitment to *Chi* is the focal point of that mission statement: Advancing knowledge is at the center of our business objectives. It is worth emphasizing that this statement was not imposed on our company by management. It grew out of a yearlong exploration of our shared values and goals that involved all of our staff, regardless of nationality, language, culture, or location. By consensus, and by passionate commitment, the advancement of *Chi* is our identity.

We strongly believe that people wish to be more productive, and they need products to assist them toward that goal. We create these products, and we can do so only at high levels of quality and profitability by constantly advancing our knowledge—and not simply our knowledge of the technical attributes of our products. That is one reason that we took a leadership role in establishing The Aspen Institute Japan in 1998.

**Breaking Barriers**

Japanese companies have traditionally been very good at generating knowledge. But entrenched hierarchies, combined with geographical and cultural boundaries, have often kept them from putting the knowledge they generate at the disposal of the whole organization. Today, all companies need to expand abroad and develop creative corporate cultures to remain competitive. My goal is to break down the barriers of rank, function, and geography that prevent ideas from spreading. To that end, we need to develop a new Japanese management model, which combines the best of Anglo-American with Japanese approaches.

We have begun this task at Fuji Xerox. We started with respect—respect for knowledge, for *Chi*—and regard that as an unshakable value. At the same time, we created what we call *spaces*, where knowledge can be exchanged freely, where employees and customers alike can become wiser. In Japanese we have a word, *Ba*, which might loosely be translated as this kind of space.

At our company we think of *Ba* as shared spaces for nurturing the creation of knowledge. These spaces may be physical, such as research and development laboratories, which have always been devoted to learning. They may be virtual spaces, such as intranets and e-mail, in which people can communicate. And they are also mental—an attitude, a climate, in which the exchange of ideas can take place freely, without expectations of application or profit. Above all, these *Ba* support *Chi*.

The challenge now is to work with these elements of our culture to generate tools that facilitate the visibility and accessibility of the collective wisdom of Fuji Xerox. Some tools will harness primarily explicit knowledge. For example, we have created the Virtual Office—a series of databases that highlights details on markets and clients, as well as stored proposals—for our marketing personnel in Japan. It also gives our sales representatives information, such as a client's use of Fuji Xerox office equipment, industry trends, corporate affiliations, and R&D efforts. As a result, the Virtual Office gives our employees tools to create their own sales approaches to their clients.

Closer to the area of tacit knowledge, with its priceless component of human exchange, is a program called "Talknade" (a compound word from "talk" and "promenade"), which was launched in the mid-1980s. It is a way of getting people together with others from all levels and areas to speak their minds. Here we are trying to do something that sounds simple but is in fact difficult and rarely attempted: to increase the extent to which people use their minds in highly innovative ways to improve our products and better serve our customers.

The whole idea of Talknade is to encourage people to exchange informally about serious subjects. Previously, when we brought groups of people together, we would oblige them to arrive with prepared data and statements—you needed definite ideas and plans. There is nothing wrong with that. But we recognized the need to create a *Ba* at an early stage in the creative process, an informal space that fosters interaction between clear-cut knowhow and tacit knowledge.

## The Heart of Our Business Philosophy

The Talknade program varies in size, composition, and theme. Senior management is always present. We try to encourage informal but clear exchanges of ideas. When I was the president of Fuji Xerox, the largest Talknade group we assembled was some 200 people, who spent the whole day in something like a dozen or more teams engaged in informal exchange.

The last few talks, under President Sakamoto's direction, have been clearly centered on our Japanese motto, *Kokomade Yarunoka Xerox*, which translates loosely as "Xerox, you do this much for me!" Literally it means, "We will do anything for our customers." It places customers at the heart of our business philosophy.

We have had some interesting results from Talknades, which further our wish to blend the best of Japanese and Western wisdom into a new company intelligence. As a result of Talknades, we introduced a new flextime scheme for our employees, created a women's committee to make sure that we are being responsive to all of our workforce, and created a venture fund that allows our people to develop their own business concepts and spin them off into affiliated companies. These may not seem new ideas in the West, but they are still rare practices in Asia.

As a result of Talknades, we have set up a special type of customer center, a final gate where our customers can speak to us when all other channels for service in the company have somehow failed to satisfy them. It functions best to help the customer and to help us understand how well our services are being used.

Best of all, as Talknade continues, tacit knowledge sharing is creating interesting chemistry among people of different expertise and functions within R&D and headquarters. It is producing solutions that would be unattainable through a rigidly logical scientific approach. It is leading to new *Ba*, such as satellite offices, located between our main offices and equipped with a full technology infrastructure, Internet access, and the library. In Japan, where the commute to work can take as long as two hours each way, these satellite offices promote work-life balance and increased productivity.

Another program intended to harness tacit knowledge is our employee rotation exchange with Xerox in the United States. Some years ago, all of the Xerox partners agreed to work more closely together. We launched joint projects. Exchanges of personnel and an evolving communication process reinforced research collaboration. Fuji Xerox people spent time as residents at Xerox, and engineers from both companies frequently crossed the Pacific to provide on-the-spot assistance.

These exchanges are also an important channel for technology transfer between the companies. Typically, about ten people from the United States or Europe come to Fuji Xerox, while about 90 of our people from Asia go to Xerox offices around the globe.

### The Payoffs

Obviously, it's difficult to measure precisely how these efforts are paying off. That is why some CEOs question their value. We certainly see change in the ways people interact with each other and in the ways that new products, services, and solutions are created and shared within the company.

There is no question that we are achieving higher productivity, and I believe that we are creating better products for our customers. We are working with one of the largest Japanese electronic and entertainment companies to help it develop global solutions for office documentation. For another client, a large automotive company, we are working with its people to manage a vast library of operational manuals. Groups from the United States, Europe, and Japan have joined us in this project to disseminate the new solutions across the client's global organization.

This collaboration occurred as a result of our global account management process, and it involved everyone from the CEO down. The solutions combine technology, alterations in work environment, and human factors. And many companies are now benchmarking this as a best practice.

As these examples make clear, we are making the transition from a commodity business to a company with knowledge-based, integrated values to offer our customers. And this is where the payoff is. If you can offer your customers the benefits of your knowledge, you enrich them and at the same time enrich your company. That mutual benefit is the goal, and knowledge is the means. ■

Excerpted from **"Wisdom of the CEO: 29 Global Leaders Tackle Today's Most Pressing Business Challenges"** by G. William Dauphinais, Grady Means, and Colin Price. Copyright 2000 by PricewaterhouseCoopers LLP. Published by John Wiley & Sons, Inc. All rights reserved.

# Online Resources

- **Featured companies**
Fuji Xerox Co., Ltd.
http://www.fujixerox.co.jp

The Aspen Institute
http://www.aspeninst.org/

- **Related article**
"Get Smart"
By Bronwyn Fryer
Many companies are profiting from combining business processes with technology to create a collective corporate memory.
http://www.inc.com/articles/details/0,3532,ART13542_CNT53,00.html

- **Related Web site**
WWW Virtual Library on Knowledge Management
This site, considered the largest collection of knowledge management literature by *The Wall Street Journal*, features forums, articles, magazines, events, resources, analyses, and news.
http://www.brint.com/km/

# Rx for Sick— and Healthy—Companies

## Michael Teng

*Managing Director, West Pharmaceutical Services Singapore*
*Singapore*

"To keep the corporate doctor away, take three meals—vision (breakfast), feedback (lunch), and action (dinner)—a day."

**Michael Teng**

Michael Teng deserves to be called a "turnaround manager." He has rescued two troubled companies—first, a Singaporean company, then a multinational firm—from near financial collapse. And he accomplished both turnarounds within his first year as general manager of each company.

To bring these companies back from the brink, the 46-year-old Teng treated each one like a sick person. As reported in *The Straits Times*, one company had serious management and operational problems. So Teng performed "surgery" and cut off the diseased parts—non-performing staff and business units. The other had people management problems and an inappropriate corporate culture. So he "resuscitated" it by using fresh strategies. Then he "rehabilitated" it by changing its culture.

In this article, adapted from an article written by Teng for *Today's Manager* magazine and a presentation he delivered before several professional organizations, he elaborates on management principles which can benefit not only ailing companies but even healthy ones.

A company falls sick just like a person does. There is a strong parallel between physical health and fiscal health. Companies can suffer from internal and external viral attacks. The former may take the form of a major project failure, incompetent management, or poor financial control. The latter includes government intervention, economic recessions, the presence of low-cost competitors, or natural disasters.

To extend the analogy, the turnaround manager acts like a doctor while a financial institution functions like a hospital. When a company experiences financial collapse—death—it is turned over to a receiver, the company's undertaker.

When a company falls seriously sick, it needs to undergo three phases to heal itself: surgery, to restructure the organization to deal with the new and harsh realities; resuscitation, to revitalize the business to improve on its sales revenues; and nursing, to rehabilitate a healthy corporate culture for sustained long-term growth.

In a corporate turnaround process, mere surgery is insufficient. Resuscitation alone is also inadequate. You can have the best resuscitation strategies but it will come to naught if your people are not behind you.

For a complete healing of a corporate illness, nursing—i.e., building a healthy corporate culture and winning the people's mindset and heart— is critical. The soft issues in nursing are just as important as dealing with the hard issues of surgery and resuscitation in a corporate rescue. A healthy corporate culture is the immunity system of the company that keeps viruses and diseases at bay.

### Surgery

There are four Cs in the first phase of a corporate turnaround: Communication, Cost control, Cash flow, and Concentration.

*Communication.* Communicate regularly with your staff, customers, board members, suppliers, and bankers on your turnaround plan and update them on the progress made. Articulate clearly ideas and procedures using unambiguous language.

People are not against bad news per se but they want to see results quickly. Get the bad news over as quickly as possible. Also, openly share credit for success with other members of the turnaround team.

*Cost control.* Remember that any first-year business student can cut costs. The difference is that a good turnaround manager is one who reduces costs without further hurting the sick company.

Avoid the "corporate anorexia" syndrome practiced by some companies which literally starves the corporations to death. Sweeping cost cutting is tempting, but it will hurt in the long run if it is not properly planned. During the cost reduction exercise to bring overheads in line with realistic levels, remember to set a good example yourself by not spending unnecessarily.

*Cash flow.* Most troubled companies require immediate improvements in cash flow. Watch your balance sheet items. Start control of inventory levels, outstanding debts, currency exchange, payments to suppliers, collection of receivables, and the like. The basic principle is "look after the pennies, and the pounds will look after themselves."

*Concentration.* Focus the troubled company on its core competencies. Troubled companies usually stray from day-to-day operational issues into acquisition and poorly thought-out expansion programs. As Jack Welch, chairman of General Electric, once said, "If you are not number one or two in the business, you will increasingly find it very difficult to survive in business today." Work on laser-sharp focus in your industry and divest non-related businesses.

## Resuscitation

Surgery is not sufficient in a corporate turnaround process. The company needs to be further resuscitated. In this phase, I recommend the following steps:

- Ascertain corporate objectives. Ensure that everyone is working toward common goals.
- Obtain support from shareholders and all business associates. Constantly keep them informed on the progress made. Without the support of these people, the turnaround manager will face an uphill battle.
- Implement aggressive marketing strategies. At one company I turned around, I implemented an aggressive ISO 9000 program. This program steered the staff away from playing the game of shame and blame, and directed their energies toward constructive activities.

- Conduct market research. We started talking to suppliers, customers, and even competitors to better understand the industry. This process included rejecting past market assumptions that got the company into trouble in the first place.
- Get the right product at the right cost. We successfully implemented multisourcing to make cheaper products available to the price-sensitive market.

### Nursing

Phase three involves the following steps: incorporating a new corporate philosophy; instilling a strong corporate culture; and increasing communication and training to reinforce the corporate philosophy and culture. A company without the right corporate philosophy and culture will still fail in the long term even if all its resuscitation strategies (phase two) are in order.

A *new corporate philosophy*. In ancient Chinese medical tradition, it is believed that a person will be healthy if he or she can release the internal energy, or *qi*. Similarly, in corporations, human resource energy should flow freely and not become blocked.

Today, businesses are getting very competitive. The key to corporate success is to learn our mistakes faster. To accomplish this, I encouraged the free flow of ideas and new ways of doing things to establish the new corporate philosophy.

Even our project management philosophy was changed. The former philosophy consisted of starting with enthusiasm, disillusionment and panic, hunting for the guilty, punishing the innocent, and rewarding non-participants. The new philosophy emphasizes a "ready, shoot, aim" strategy and views project management as a continuing process of trial and failure.

A *healthy corporate culture*. In today's competitive market, it is difficult to differentiate your products and services based on technology or pricing alone. But if your company has a healthy corporate culture, it will take a long while for your competitors to follow.

*Communication and training*. Both are needed to support the new corporate philosophy. As the CEO, I communicated with staff at training sessions, team briefings, and informal gatherings.

Ken Blanchard, author of *The One-Minute Manager*, once said that feedback is the breakfast of champions. However, I believe that in the communication process, vision is breakfast, i.e., without the healthy corporate philosophy, the company's efforts can be derailed. Feedback is lunch. And acting on the feedback is dinner.

Many corporations receive feedback reports but are not able to act on them. Vision, feedback, and action are the three meals a day that will keep the corporate doctor away.

Training and development are other important aspects of the nursing stage. I trained my team managers, as change agents, to assist me in instilling a more positive mindset among the staff. Increased training resulted in an added benefit: It resulted in engendering staff loyalty and reducing staff attrition.

Turnaround situations can be difficult. If you take too long to show results, staff members get impatient. Bankers withdraw your credit line when they smell trouble in your company. Even bosses and shareholders give you little margin for error.

Overall, managing a turnaround is a trying and rewarding experience. Ultimately, it is nothing magical, but simply a matter of going back to the basics. ■

---

First published in **Today's Manager**, the official publication of the Singapore Institute of Management.

The biographical sketch was drawn using the following sources:
"Men Who Turn Red into Black." *The Straits Times:* March 16, 1996.
Dayao, Dinna Louise C. "Rx for Sick—and Healthy—Companies." *World Executive's Digest:* October 1997.

# Online Resources

- **Featured company**
  West Pharmaceutical Services
  http://www.westpharma.com/

- **Related articles**
  "Reforms—the Key to Survival"
  By the editors of *Asiaweek* magazine
  Cost cutting, restructuring, and forays into the new economy. That's how these companies overcame the Asian crisis.
  http://www.cnn.com/ASIANOW/asiaweek/magazine/2000/0714/cs.reform.html

  "Corps Values"
  By David H. Freedman
  The U.S. Marines are trained to make split-second decisions based on incomplete information, in life-or-death situations. Can they provide clues to running a faster-reacting business?
  http://www.inc.com/incmagazine/archives/04980541.html

# PART 5

# MARKETING AND CUSTOMER SERVICE STRATEGIES

# The Seven Deadly Sins of Service Management

*Peter Lau*

*Chairman and CEO, Giordano International Ltd.*
*Hong Kong SAR*

"Customer service ranges from the 'minimums,' which include staff courtesy and an exchange policy, to the 'invisibles,' really solving customer problems."

**Peter Lau**

In the last few years, Giordano International Ltd. has been dogged by many concerns. First, its founder and former head Jimmy Lai's criticism of China stalled the company's expansion into the mainland and undermined its reputation as a darling of foreign investors. Then, as the Asian crisis hit Hong Kong SAR's tourist traffic, the T-shirt trade dried up. After Peter Lau, 48, took over as chairman and chief executive in 1994, sales leapt—but only briefly.

That was then. While competing retailers struggle to ride out Asia's recession, Lau took advantage of the crisis to take out weak links. Repositioning the company within a market where consumers have become more discriminating, he steered Giordano toward a new emphasis on sensible but stylish clothes. In China, Lau shut down the company's main factory and started outsourcing in countries that have depreciated currencies. He also managed the balance sheet prudently, specifically by building an inventory management culture involving Giordano's buyers, warehouse people, and salespeople.

Lau's strategies have paid off: Giordano's 1998 sales rose to US$336.8 million, 13.4% more than the previous year's, while net income grew to US$9.8 million, up by 11.9% from 1997. His continued efforts to upgrade quality, keep up with new styles, and relentlessly cut costs boosted sales at the casual-wear retailer by 20% in 1999 to US$400 million.

Lau may have redefined Giordano by implementing new systems, but the company's customer service philosophy remains the same throughout the more than 670 stores in Asia, New Zealand, and the Middle East, where the retail chain operates or have franchises. Giordano keeps customers happy by first focusing on employee satisfaction. Aside from its policy of paying employees

10% to 15% above-market salaries, crisis or no crisis, Giordano conducts annual employee attitude surveys yearly. In the latest survey, employee satisfaction rated 3.02 out of a four-point scale.

In this article, adapted from a presentation that Lau delivered to Giordano staff and customer service experts alike, he cautions against the seven deadly sins of service management.

M ost companies pay lip service to customer service. At Giordano, we believe that customers drive our business and that customer service is the key to our company's survival. The difference lies in our ability to build and sustain high standards of customer service.

Outstanding customer service is a cornerstone of Giordano's success. We cannot afford to be complacent. Sustaining high levels of customer service is the real test of the company's systems.

Apart from preaching from the highest possible level, there needs to be a company-wide system to support the levels of service, which range from the "minimums," which include staff courtesy and an exchange policy, to the "invisibles," really solving customer problems. In delivering customer service, the frontline is primarily responsible for the minimums and the management for the invisibles.

Following is a list of the seven deadly sins of service management and how Giordano avoids committing them.

### Sin #1: Short-sightedness

Instead of calculating the immediate economic return of each service initiative, Giordano focuses on each initiative's long-term cumulative returns. Instead of focusing on nickels and dimes, we'd rather emphasize how our policies are helping us adhere to our business principles of offering value for money, simplicity, quality, and supreme customer service.

## Sin #2: Unhappy Frontliners

Frontline employees serve paying customers, but who serves the frontline? If they are underpaid and overworked, frontline employees will suffer from low self-esteem and will not perform to the best of their abilities. Unhappy service staff will result in unhappy customers.

At Giordano, we have been offering our frontliners a one-and-a-half day holiday weekly since 1988. We were among the first to provide this benefit. Our frontliners are also constantly given "attitude training," including a two-day personal growth off-site workshop.

## Sin #3: Bloated Management Ego

Most managers believe that they know better than their staff and customers. We believe in sharing information.[1] Every morning, the *Giordano Morning Post*, which lists information such as each shop's sales and which items sell well, is faxed to all shops.

Management pays attention to the customers' suggestions obtained from surveys and a "mystery shopper" program. In 1998, we implemented a program to solicit suggestions from customers and promised to reward each suggestion with a free Giordano T-shirt. The program was a huge success—20,000 T-shirts were given out.

We don't believe that memos can take the place of coaching. Every morning, at each store, store managers brief their staff before opening for business.

---

[1] Giordano managers have much reason to listen to their staff. The company's employees take the initiative in cutting overhead and administrative costs, reports *Chief Executive Asia* magazine. In one brainstorming session, they suggested changing from paper shopping bags to recyclable plastic bags, which saves almost 60% on the cost of bags. Employees have even identified unnecessary benefits. In another brainstorming session, they found out that it cost HK$200,000 a year to maintain the contract on a vacation house Giordano kept in one of the outlying islands of Hong Kong SAR and suggested the company terminate it.

## Sin #4: Absence of Customer-Friendly Policies

Most companies have procedures that are designed for their own protection, but not for the satisfaction of their customers. Our company policies facilitate rather than inhibit good customer service. Giordano's exchange policy, which is generally "no questions asked," is liberal, as is our refund policy. Our store staff are empowered to implement both policies to the best of their judgment.

## Sin #5: Training for Short-Term Returns
## Rather than for Character Building

Many companies do not have holistic people-development programs. Giordano trains employees not only in selling skills but also in personal skills. Employees attend personal growth workshops. For the past three years, we have been devoting an average of HK$5,465 training dollars per employee and 34 training hours per employee.

Aware of the shortage of skilled management talent in Asia, we take a long-term view to succession planning. We are recruiting 150 university graduates as trainees in a two-year program. These young trainees will form our management backbone in the years 2001 to 2006.

## Sin #6: Management Doesn't Walk the Talk

Most managers fail to lead by example. All Giordano senior managers frequent our stores. They openly and frequently communicate with sales staff. Store managers are encouraged to actually talk to Giordano customers and obtain information firsthand, instead of letting sales associates do all the work. We believe in the power of direct communication so that we can learn from our customers.

Lastly, all company policies apply to all employees equally. No extra privilege is given to anybody—even I don't get discounts without the required discount coupons.

## Sin #7: Complacency

No strategic plan in the world can anticipate sudden changes in the operating environment. We must build our preparedness to adapt to crises and grab opportunities.

So instead of being satisfied with the status quo, we constantly seek ways to improve our processes for anticipating and fulfilling customer demands.[2] To stay abreast of fashion trends, for example, our New York design studio sends us the latest in fashion basics from the United States via the Internet. We have begun to sell our products through our Web site and invite customers to rate our service by replying to an online survey. ■

The biographical sketch was drawn using the following sources:

Kazmin, Amy Louise. "Giordano Comes in from the Cold." *Business Week:* May 31, 1998.

Lau, Peter. "The Goal Is Not to Recover, But to Redefine." *Chief Executive Asia:* November 1998.

The correspondents and editors of *Business Week.* "The Stars of Asia: 50 Leaders at the Forefront of Change." *Business Week,* July 3, 2000.

---

[2] Lau is also testing new ideas, such as Giordano Ladies, reports *Business Week* magazine. The boutique chain, which Lau describes as a "kind of laboratory," sells clothing lines that are trendier and a notch up the price scale from Giordano shops.

## Online Resources

- **Featured company**
  Giordano International Limited
  http://www.giordano.com.hk/giordano/home1.html

- **Related articles**
  "The Cycle of Service: How to See Things
  from the Customer's Point of View"
  By Steven Albrecht
  When customers come to your company, they are guided by service histories,
  life experiences, and recommendations from others. To go where the
  customer goes, you need a special kind of map—the Cycle of Service—to
  help both of you get to your destination, a quality service experience.
  http://www.smartbiz.com/sbs/arts/sss1.htm

  "The Definitive Handbook for Great Customer Service"
  By the editors of *Fast Company*
  A comprehensive guide to listening to, working with, and learning from the
  most important person in our business—the customer!
  http://www.fastcompany.com/fc/service/index.html
  http://www.fastcompany.com/fc/service/index.html

# Making Quality Service
# a Way of Life

*Deepak S. Parekh*

Chairman, Housing Development Finance Corporation
India

"Service management is the yardstick that measures the efficiency with which HDFC designs and delivers products to its customers."

**Deepak S. Parekh**

Deepak S. Parekh is consistently cited among annual lists of India's best CEOs. And with good reason: The 56-year-old chairman of Housing Development Finance Corporation (HDFC) is known for his role in creating and expanding India's home mortgage market, earning the gratitude of more than one million middle-class homeowners. HDFC is now a financial conglomerate with assets of US$2.5 billion, and its annual earnings are rising steadily at double-digit rates.

HDFC's prospects didn't always look so rosy. In 1998, when HDFC won a Qimpro Platinum award, which is given to practitioners of quality in corporate India, Parekh admitted in his acceptance speech that he sometimes wondered how HDFC succeeded against formidable odds: "What was in effect being established in 1978 was a financial institution intending to finance households directly—which no institution in the country had dared to do on any scale— and service the loans efficiently, in the absence of any legally practicable way of foreclosing on mortgages."

How did HDFC overcome these odds to grow into one of India's most respected financial services companies, offering services ranging from banking and consumer finance to infrastructure? By making quality service the cornerstone which predicates everything the company does—from product development to training—and implementing systems to ensure that the company continuously meets customers' increasingly high expectations.

In this article, which is adapted from the 1998 acceptance speech and based in part on an interview conducted by Dinna Louise C. Dayao, Parekh describes HDFC's service management philosophy.

I t is a great honor to be the first ever recipient of the Qimpro Platinum Standard from the service sector. The very baseline of Qimpro, "making quality improvements a way of life," defines the essence of doing business in a global marketplace characterized by a competitive economy, the presence of more players, and quality-conscious customers.

All of these factors require a new strategy of businesses with respect to customer retention. Customers with higher and rising expectations will be less loyal and will seek convenience, speed, and service quality at competitive prices. Ultimately, it will be the service quality that we can deliver that will result in the retention of customers.

At HDFC, we decided to reengineer on the basis of the customer once we took the crucial decision to tap retail markets on both sides of the balance sheet—we make loans to individuals as well as accept deposits from households. HDFC currently deals with over 1.5 million households on a regular basis. Thus, we need a clear customer service strategy in this crucial area.

Fortunately, the transition was not painful for us, as we have throughout our history behaved as if we faced a competitive market. From the very first day we opened our doors for business in 1978, we have developed our products, our staff, and our systems with one unified theme—to provide the best customer service we could possibly offer. As a result, we have always been equipped with a state-of-the-art system, a highly trained office staff, and an organizational framework in place to face a competitive environment.

Still, the advent of increased competition has forced us to further finetune our skills. We have adopted a comprehensive approach to service management, which I would now like to outline.

### Meeting Rising Expectations

HDFC's service reputation has always been high, but this only breeds complacency. Knowing why one is succeeding and managing that process is the essence of sustainable success, and without participative management the process simply will not work.

Let me explain: When customers enter HDFC's offices for the first time, they bring expectations formed through their experiences with other inferior service organizations. At HDFC, they experience professional service. At this point in time, they experience customer delight because the service they received exceeded their expectations.

The next time they enter our offices, their expectation is based not on the level of service experienced at other institutions but on their experience with HDFC on their last visit. At this point, customer delight is replaced by customer satisfaction. Customers expect to receive quality service and their expectations are met.

The next time customers visit the HDFC office, they may even experience customer dissatisfaction as their expectations now exceed service delivery. Interestingly, while HDFC's level of service may not have undergone any change, customer delight has been transformed to customer dissatisfaction.

Therefore, how does one improve service when service demands are continuously rising? By measuring the change in customer expectations and then responding to it by continual and sustained improvement of service standards. Service management is the yardstick that measures the efficiency with which HDFC designs and delivers products to its customers.

Thanks to our service management philosophy, we are winning the customer service game. The substantial growth in our retail deposit base—from 50,000 depositors in 1991 to over 1 million in 1998—is almost entirely due to the sustained service delivery mechanisms in place for our deposit agents and depositors.

At HDFC, service management has been systematically built into the organization over the years and the endeavor continues. From the beginning, HDFC's strategies for designing innovative products and services, delivering service, and training staff have been shaped by the image HDFC wanted to create in the mind of the customer—an institution which would fulfill the customer's needs with a human face.

## Designing Products with the Customer in Mind

The design, development, and introduction of new HDFC products and services have been completely predicated by customer requirements. For example, when HDFC noticed that many of its loan applicants were young professionals, who were eligible for small loans on the basis of their current income but could earn many times more in the future, we launched a step-up loan repayment facility. Under this facility, loan repayments are structured to keep up with the increase in the salary of the professional. Similarly, we launched a step-down facility to accommodate the needs expressed by a father-and-son or elderly-husband-and-wife team, where the father or husband would be retiring before the expiry of the complete term of the loan.

With the steady downward movement in interest rates over the past year, HDFC received requests from existing borrowers for interest rate reductions on their home loans. At the same time, we also received inquiries from customers to prepay loans availed at higher rates of interest using refinance options being made available by banks and other housing finance companies. In response to this customer feedback, HDFC now offers its customers a choice between an adjustable rate loan and a fixed rate loan.

## Sharing Best Practices

HDFC has been consistently refining the operational processes within the organization. The process of refinement has undergone various stages, including staff training, setting up teams for reviewing existing processes, in-house feedback systems, and process mapping.

We have set up inter-branch teams comprising operating staff to study the best practices in different branches and recommend implementation across the company. These teams have helped highlight local best practices, which can be implemented in a more effective manner. To make experience sharing easier across the company, we established an in-house magazine to provide a forum for all branches to share the innovative practices, which were tested and implemented at respective locations.

HDFC has implemented uniform automated systems across all branches throughout India. We have mapped out the ideal lending process to ensure uniformity in implementation and service standards. These process maps are discussed with the operating staff at every branch. Any deviation from the ideal process, provided it improves customer service, will be incorporated. Once all branches operate within a uniform framework, we can prescribe and monitor service standards.

## Managing Cycle Time

From the design of forms to HDFC's lending policy, we are concerned with the process being efficient and cost-effective, both to the customer as well as to the organization. For example, in the early years, the loan approval process was highly centralized. All loan applications were recommended by the branches but approved only at the head office. As a result, turnaround time for loans took four to six weeks.

To shorten the process, we set up approval committees, consisting of branch managers and officers, to approve loans up to a particular limit in the branch offices. This process also indicated our high level of confidence in the competence of branch personnel. The result: cycle time was reduced to two to four weeks.

HDFC believes in providing solutions, not just products. For example, we have established the existence of "loan counselors" to educate walk-in customers about the aspects related to acquiring a house, including the loan application process and legal formalities. Loan counselors do not only help improve customer service; they also help reduce cycle time and convert inquiries into loan applications.

Currently, if a customer submits his or her application and all the papers are in order, HDFC can immediately offer the customer a loan letter and disbursement check. This is possible because loan applications are no longer processed by three different employees from the credit, legal, and technical departments. The credit and legal appraisal functions are now assigned only to one person and the information flow on the system, including the technical status of the property being financed, was reorganized. To facilitate this, credit appraisers and legal appraisers were cross-trained. Also, seating arrangements of the staff were planned to provide maximum communication between them as they interact with customers.

## How Training Provides a Common Service Platform

At HDFC, staff training in service delivery moves through four different stages. Each stage provides a common platform for staff to discuss service-related issues among cross-functional teams, thereby enabling staff to not only acquire appropriate skills, but also to achieve a higher level of understanding of HDFC's products and processes.

Stage 1, a workshop on customer relations, looks at attitudes and behavior through a skill model for customer relations. The skills discussed include welcoming the customer, communicating with the customer, and managing dissatisfied customers.

Stage 2, a workshop on "HDFC, Service, and You," looks at HDFC's interactions with customers from the customer's perspective to ensure that appropriate strategies are adopted to maximize the quality of the interaction. The workshop's objectives are developing empathy with customers and their experience of HDFC's service; identifying specific "moments of truth" that require improvement; and preparing a plan of action for improving the customer's experience.

Stage 3, a Quest workshop, provides branch-level teams with a systematic approach and tools—including Pareto analysis, fishbone diagrams, and process mapping—to diagnose service delivery gaps and identify practical solutions.

Stage 4, a workshop on "Enhancing Personal Effectiveness," is designed to empower participants to be fully in control of their lives and optimize their unlimited potential, thereby enabling them to achieve breakthroughs at work as well as in their personal lives. The program's objectives include enabling participants to detect their mission in life, create commitment, and set short- and long-term targets, and helping the participant to understand the principles and techniques of dealing with his family members, peers, and bosses, thus enabling him to be effective personally as well as professionally.

The future of business in a competitive global economy will increasingly depend on our ability to deliver our products and services in an efficient and cost-effective manner. Service then becomes a prerequisite for survival. HDFC has taken this to heart and is implementing—and succeeding—through a careful concentration on managing service to adhere to quality standards and show its concern for the customer. ■

The biographical sketch was drawn using the following sources:

Radhakrishnann, N. "The Making of a Financial Powerhouse." *Business India:* August 16-29, 1993.

The editors of *Business Week.* "Stars of Asia." *Business Week:* June 29, 1998.

## Online Resources

- **Featured company**
  Housing Development Finance Corporation
  http://www.hdfc.com

- **Related articles**
  "Build Loyal Advocates!"
  By Mike Keleher
  In the Internet era, a dissatisfied customer can instantly tell thousands of people about perceived mistreatment. In this environment, leaders must establish the people, processes, technology, and expectations to build loyal advocates.
  http://www.mgeneral.com/3-now/99-now/051999mk.htm

  "First Line of Defense"
  By Rochelle Garner
  At SBC Communications, an onslaught of customer calls led to the adoption of Web-based tools. While not perfect, the tools are giving service a boost.
  http://www.cio.com/archive/webbusiness/120199_sbc.html

  "Service Encounters of the Third Kind™"
  By Ron Kaufman
  What characterizes the service relationship between companies and customers who do business together for decades, even centuries?
  http://www.ronkaufman.com/articles/article.3rdkind.html

# Marketing in East Asia:
# The Fallacies and the Realities

*Ralph Kugler*

*Latin America Business Group President, Unilever*
*United Kingdom*

"To understand trends in Asian consumption, we need to extinguish some myths. Successful brands can only grow out of a deep understanding of Asian consumer attitudes and behavior."

**Ralph Kugler**

Ralph Kugler, 45, joined Unilever in 1979 and has worked in six subsidiaries in five countries in Africa, Latin America, and East Asia since then. He was appointed chairman and CEO of Unilever in Malaysia in 1992 and chairman and CEO of Unilever Thai Holdings in 1995. As the first chairman of the Efficient Consumer Response (ECR) Board of Thailand from 1998 to 1999, Kugler is playing a leading role in the introduction of ECR in Thailand. In 1999, he was appointed Latin America Business Group president.

T he crisis in East Asia has prompted many questions about the tiger economies and their consumers: Is it reasonable to talk of East Asian people as a single, homogeneous group? Is it sufficient to focus on urban middle-class consumers, to understand the most important consumer trends? How are East Asian consumers changing? What will be the long-term impact of the economic downturn?

To compound these myths, East Asia is the source of many misconceptions. Are the countries First or Third World? Have the 8% to 10% growth rates of the tiger economies been built on systematic development, or are they just the result of foreign investment? Do the middle classes, with their growing affluence, increasingly resemble Westerners in their consumer behavior?

To understand trends in Asian consumption, we need to extinguish some of these myths.

## Myth #1: There Is One Asia

There are many Asias. Differences reflect race, religion and culture (from Islam to Buddhism, from Confucianism to Shintoism), income, and levels of sophistication.

## Myth #2: National Populations Are Homogeneous

Behaviors and attitudes reflect income and social class more than nationality. For example, there may be more similarities between the urban populations of Malaysia, Thailand, and Taiwan than within each country alone. The incomes of urban consumers in Tokyo and Singapore are up to one hundred times higher than their rural counterparts.

The Overseas Chinese are a unifying factor. They can be found in cities throughout East Asia, and are highly influential in running business and in consumption patterns. Discrete Chinese communities have more in common between them than, for instance, Muslim neighbors on a Kuala Lumpur street do. Hence, the Chinese TV series, "Pao Boon Jin" ("made in Taiwan") is popular throughout the region.

## Myth #3: The Only Consumers Worth Considering Are the Middle Classes

This is an urban prejudice. The middle class is growing, but the bulk of consumption is still among lower-income consumers and will continue to be so for many years.

To understand Asian consumers, one must leave the cities. Visitors to Thailand typically see Bangkok and Phuket, then generalize about the country as a whole; but while washing machine ownership is nearly 50% in Bangkok, it is less than 10% in the rest of the country.

## Myth #4: Affluent Asians Are Becoming Westernized in Tastes and Behavior

A more affluent Asia will not become a West in the East. There are important differences in culture and behavior. Western society is more individualist, while Asian behavior is more collectivist. Face continues to be a factor explaining Asian consumer behavior.

The extent to which East Asian consumers will become Westernized is limited. It is true that young Asians are more influenced by Western style; that more women are going to work; and that the retail scene is rapidly changing, driven by the arrival of European and American retail chains. However, consumer changes remain within the cultural context of Asia, and attitudes are distinct from those found in the West. Tokyo is more affluent than many advanced countries, but no more Western than sumo and sashimi.

## Myth #5: The Boom Has Ended

The crisis in East Asia will impede the rate of development; but it is not likely to change the direction of market evolution. Consumer behavior already acquired will not be unlearned. By 2000, the more competitive Asian economies will probably return to attractive rates of expansion.

Urban consumers are undergoing rapid changes, but within the existing cultural framework. The nuclear family receives greater emphasis than in the past, but allegiance to the extended family continues. Materialism is growing rapidly.

Culture may take inspiration from the West. The arrival of satellite TV has brought aspirational Western totems. Despite this, the popular Channel V and MTV, produced in Bombay and Singapore, respectively, play mainly Asian music. Western bands are not popular despite the growth of a global teen culture.

Youth are more emancipated, but still defer to the authoritarian, paternal style of their elders. Advertising for middle-class brands—the upmarket Regent Hotel and the Thai Farmers Bank, for example—exhorts consumers to show respect and to live up to Thai values.

Young urbanites have more money to spend on themselves. American style is trendy. Nike and Levi's are widespread. But this is fashion rather than conviction. Coke and Pepsi are big brands (though note that the recipes are sweeter than in the West).

More women are going to work. They can hire relatively cheap domestic help. Asian mothers are still expected to care for their families. So while they don't necessarily clean or cook daily, they are increasingly turning to convenience products. Asian pot noodles are big. Western convenience foods have not caught on as well.

The retailing scene is changing. In Thailand, over 50% of retail purchases will be from supermarkets and hypermarkets by the year 2000, compared with under 20% in 1990. In many countries, there has been an invasion of Western retail formats.

These new retailers are increasing choice and lowering prices; but they do not reach rural markets. Thus, rural consumers will have to pay more for the same goods, effectively subsidizing the consumption of their better-off urban cousins.

Therefore, by virtue of different consumer behaviors and different retail models, two distinct groups are developing in Asia: the urban groups and the rural groups, both of which have increasingly more in common with similar groups across Asian countries.

Asian consumers are better attuned to coping with the economic downturn, despite no recent experience of recession. Their agrarian background means that they are used to adjusting from seasons of plenty to famine. Thrift is an important value. Asians have a high propensity to save.

Despite the currency turmoil and economic slowdown, there continues to be great potential for growth. Asian consumption levels are still low and there is a strong consumerist culture.

Successful brands can only grow out of a deep understanding of Asian consumer attitudes and behavior. Transferring Western mixes is by no means a certain recipe for success. One of Wall's Ice Cream's biggest successes in the region has been Asian Delight, a coconut-based ice cream with local ingredients like red bean and yam. Häagen Dazs has had a big hit in Japan with a new Green Tea variant.

Asian and Western consumers are not and will not be the same. The Asian way is collectivist, the Western is individualist. Western styles and tastes cannot be automatically transplanted to Asia, unless they reflect real changes of attitude or fashion. The successful multinational typically brings its brands, quality, and technology, but adapts product mixes to local Asian tastes.

Asian consumers are evolving rapidly. They have a desire for ostentatious consumption of the world's most expensive brands. But whether it is a housewife searching for more convenience or a teenager buying a Lacoste shirt, their attitudes remain bound up in the paternal, collectivist tradition in which they were brought up.

Finally, despite the crisis, Asian consumers will not unlearn the benefits of better-quality goods that they have moved to. They will not regress to rejected habits and products. Brand loyalty will increase, for brands that offer improved value and relevant innovations.

In conclusion, Asia will soon be the world's largest market, incorporating the megaliths of China, Japan, and Southeast Asia. The potential is huge, but it is greatest for those who understand the attitudes, needs, and behaviors of Asians, and the market triggers and barriers. ■

---

This paper was first published in **The Journal of Brand Management** (www.henrystewart.com/journals/BM/), pp. 194-199, Volume 5, Number 3, in January 1998; Henry Stewart Publications, London, U.K.

## Online Resources

- **Featured company**
  Unilever Plc
  http://www.unilever.com

- **Related articles**
  "Consuming Passions"
  By Joanna Slater
  The promise of 1.2 billion consumers has mostly been a mirage for foreign companies seeking to make a fortune in China. Food company Pillsbury is counting on extensive, carefully crafted marketing to lead its charge into this new territory.
  http://203.105.48.72/9903_18/p46marketing.html

  "The Long March"
  By Trish Saywell
  Chinese brands have ample potential to go global, but there's still a lengthy road to travel. Building a brand takes money and marketing skills, which are in short supply.
  http://203.105.48.72/9901_14/p66marketing.html

# Debunking the Myths
# of Advertising

*Emily Abrera*

Chairman and CEO, McCann-Erickson Philippines
Philippines

"Advertising is hard work. The best of us hold ourselves fully accountable for every centavo spent of clients' ad budgets."

**Emily Abrera**

Emily Abrera has spent more than two decades in advertising. She joined McCann-Erickson Philippines, the local office of the McCann-Erickson World Group, as a creative group head in 1978 and was named president and CEO in 1992. Advertising, she says, is the industry she "loves and thrives on and also the one that frustrates and embarrasses me often, for while there are many excellent ads, the few bad ones can be quite damaging."

Abrera need not fear for her ad agency's reputation. McCann-Erickson Philippines billed 2.2 billion pesos in 1998, making it the number one advertising agency in the Philippines, in terms of billings, for the 11th straight year. The firm has been recognized for its market performance and industry leadership and has won numerous creative awards.

Abrera, 54, credits advertising for giving her the opportunity to both learn and teach. She is an active lecturer in industry fora and the academe. In this article, which appeared in her column named "Blue Sky" for *The Evening Paper*, she describes her passion for advertising and shatters some of the myths surrounding the profession.

I'm sure every single one of you woke up this morning, had your cup of coffee, showered, dressed, read the papers, had some breakfast, maybe even popped a vitamin pill, hugged the kids, kissed the spouse, got into your car, and went to work.

Well, if you were working in an ad agency, you'd have done things quite differently.

You'd have heard your Casio alarm clock go off, sleepily shut it off, and achingly pried your body away from your Salem mattress. You'd have stretched, and then almost automatically, you'd have groped for the remote control and turned on your Sony Trinitron to the Skycable news channel, as you headed for the bathroom. You'd have reached for your Reach toothbrush, squeezed Close-up from a tube, and brushed your teeth. Then you'd have headed for the kitchen where you stirred together a steaming cup of Master Roast, Coffeemate, and Equal.

You'd have glanced at the time, your 3-D wall clock saying you're running late, so you rushed through your Safeguard shower, and worked up a lather with Rejoice, foamed up and shaved with Gillette, slicked on some Johnson's Baby Oil, and slipped into your new pair of Rockport shoes.

Then you'd have rushed down, demolishing some Campofrio Lean n' Mean Bacon with some omelet, gulped down your Enervon C for the day, and you'd have gotten into your Nissan Sentra and—this is the only time you are like everyone else—you'd crawl to work in the traffic.

There are some myths that have surrounded the noble profession of advertising, which should be shattered once and for all, although a few of the things you've heard about us are true.

For example, there's a common belief that advertising people live, eat, breathe, and even dream advertising. This is not a myth. This is true. Sometimes we even go so far as to get married to our profession. Unless an advertising person's human mate is in a similar career, this situation never works out, because they never get to see each other.

Let's get into the myths:

*Ad executives have glamorous jobs.* False.

*Ad executives have glamorous salaries.* False.

*All ad executives dress fashionably.* Ha-ha-ha. Obviously not true.

Far from being a glamorous career, advertising is hard work. We spend long hours debating details in a commercial, details that no consumer will notice anyway, and expend energy meeting, discussing, bargaining, and thinking for clients. After 8 p.m., we can devote ourselves to running our companies.

What we earn is hardly glamorous when you consider that we're on call almost 24 hours a day and usually work 12 to 15 hours anyway. Furthermore, monstrous traffic jams have increased our hours on the job, as we'd rather keep working than sit in an unmoving vehicle breathing globs of carbon monoxide.

As to being fashionably dressed, many advertising executives dress well to compensate for being broke. Advertising and creative people dress weird to ward off evil yet attract attention, make clients feel they're in the presence of magical, mystical beings, or because tradition dictates that creatives be out of touch with the mundane and the boring. They also color their hair green for the same reasons.

*Ad people have fulfilling jobs because they're creating all the time.* False. It's frustrating to get rejected eight out of ten times. Statistics say that only one out of every five of our great original ideas will coincide with the client's thinking. But you can say that we are a hardy, resilient lot because of this training.

*Awards won are the best measure of an agency's worth.* Not true. The business success of our clients and their brands is where you test how well your ad agency performs. Advertising creativity must fulfill the set objectives first; creative awards are the bonus.

*Agencies win and keep accounts on the basis of connections.* Not true. The days are long past when an agency's income was earned simply by arranging parties, playing golf, or ensuring its "connections" stayed up there in the client's hierarchy. Some persist in this belief but slowly their tribe is disappearing, and rightly so.

We are accountable daily for thinking intelligently about brands, and the best of us hold ourselves fully accountable for every centavo spent of clients' ad budgets. We want to know our ads have had an effect. But truly, we are too often seen to be only as good as our last campaign. Which is also to say that we deliver best results when we enjoy trust, friendship, loyalty, and are treated as true partners in a long-term relationship.

*Advertising is useless, serving only to push up the cost of marketing and the price of goods.* Not, not, not true.

Advertising is a valuable part of the marketing mix, and especially so in today's context because technology renders many products generic. Advertising is thus the only and the most valuable differentiator. Advertising informs consumers, improves the quality of goods offered, makes entertainment and new programming possible, and gives new brands a fighting chance, not to mention the economic force that is generated for the country.

*Ad agencies are dedicated only to the pursuit of awards and/or profit, or both.* False.

We serve a larger community of marketing professionals in the industry, citizens who deserve public space for common thought and dialogue, and a country in dire need of all the help it can get. That's why many ad agencies do pro bono work for worthy causes; that's why we embark on public service campaigns; and that is what makes us proud and happy and pleased to be in advertising. ∎

## Online Resources

- **Featured company**
  McCann-Erickson World Group
  http://www.mccann.com

- **Related article**
  "The Message Is the Marvel"
  By Lauren Heist
  Dot.com advertising has launched a creative revolution. It has created a new Renaissance for advertising.
  http://www.fastcompany.com/feature/web_ads.html

- **Related Web site**
  *Adweek Online*
  The newsweekly for the advertising industry features articles covering the latest marketing ideas, research, successful ad campaigns, graphics and creativity, and trends in media.
  http://www.adweek.com

# Winning the Customer's Heart, Mind, and Stomach

*Robert Kuan*

*Founder, Chowking Food Corporation*
*Philippines*

"We cannot afford to sit back and relax. We must stay on our toes every minute to get ahead in the marketing game."

**Robert Kuan**

When Robert Kuan opened his first Chowking restaurant in 1985 and announced his plan to run the Philippines' leading Chinese fast-food chain, few people took him seriously. The country's economy, then suffering from the mismanagement of the Marcos regime, was at its lowest point and there was widespread capital flight.

Still, Kuan, now 53, saw an opportunity to turn his dream—to be the only nationwide chain-selling reasonably priced, traditional Chinese food products in a clean, modern setting with fast service—into a reality. Armed with years of experience of managing a family-owned noodles specialty restaurant, a concept culled from his MBA thesis and marketing savvy, he has grown Chowking Food Corp., which had net sales of 1.1 billion pesos in 1998, into a dominant player in the Philippine fast-food market. (Editor's note: In 1999, Kuan sold Chowking to Jollibee Foods Corp., the Philippines' largest food chain.)

The reasons behind Chowking's success? Kuan cites three: a corporate culture which puts a premium on thrift; having the right people; and aggressive marketing. A master in the art of operating on limited resources, Kuan used secondhand roofing materials and kitchen equipment in building and furnishing Chowking's central kitchen, thereby saving millions of pesos.

Kuan did not hire executives from outside the organization, preferring instead to promote from within. He took pride in having production managers who started with Chowking as dishwashers.

Lastly, Kuan firmly believed in the power of marketing. In this article, he describes how Chowking successfully played the marketing game.

W hen we started Chowking in 1985, things were very simple. Like a parent fussing over a first-born child, we devoted time and attention to our one store. We had a basic product line that hewed closely to the offerings of a traditional Chinese noodle shop. Because we were newcomers with humble aspirations, we didn't feel pressured to elbow our way into the lion's den.

Today, 15 years later, things are considerably more complicated. With 162 outlets, including four in the United States and three in Dubai, we no longer have the luxury of time. We still carry our original menu but have since added many new products. Competition in the industry has become infinitely more heated, with new entrants boldly testing the waters and the established names digging their heels into their niches and refusing to give an inch.

Clearly, we cannot afford to sit back and relax. We must stay on our toes every minute to score points and get ahead. We know the name of the game and we know how to play it.

The game is marketing and we have a few stories to tell about how we have successfully played it to win our customer's heart, mind, and stomach.

### Targeting a New Market Segment

Traditionally, our noodle soup line enjoyed the biggest patronage during lunch and dinner times, mainly because the meals were served in a large bowl to match a big appetite and wallet. Because of its hefty tag price, it attracted only the "can-afford" crowd of office types and students of exclusive schools. And because it came in generous servings, it was considered filling enough for lunch or dinner. No one in the Chinese fast-food category thought of promoting it for meals other than the day's main meals.

In 1992, we studied the situation and saw an opportunity to offer our noodles as an alternative afternoon snack fare. We then set out to redesign the product, slightly reducing the serving portions just enough for afternoon snacks and lowering the price to make it competitive with other offerings in the market and position it within the reach of low-income customers.

We sold the new product via a massive advertising campaign which dramatically increased noodles sales by 40% in the first month and 50% in the succeeding months. Afternoon snack sales, we found, accounted for much of the increase. We also discovered that patronage of the noodle soup line by low-income customers brought in a bonus that was not entirely unexpected—an increase in *dim sum* sales. The lower price had allowed customers a side order of *dim sum*, a modest luxury.

The success of this marketing strategy shows that research and internal reports are powerful aids in attracting segments which are non-users of a certain product. Two marketing Ps—Product and Price—were changed to fit the needs of new users, while a third P, Promotion, created awareness and eventually sold the product to a new segment of the market.

### Increased Product Awareness = Increased Sales

In the last months of 1993, our product review revealed that while the Chowking *halo-halo* (literally "mix-mix," a traditional Filipino snack consisting of shaved ice, sweetened fruits, milk, and sometimes ice cream) enjoyed high acceptance among its consumers, it was not among our top ten products. After further research, we found that though the product scored high in likeability in terms of taste and pricing, it suffered in terms of consumer awareness.

*Halo-halo*, after all, was not a usual offering in a Chinese fast-food restaurant. Our challenge was to let prospective customers know that Chowking had *halo-halo* on its menu and that it was worth a try.

We developed an advertising campaign on the product and gave it heavy airtime during the summer months of 1994. It was the first time anyone had ever promoted *halo-halo* through a full-blown ad campaign. We continued the advertising blitz every summer in the succeeding years, spending a tidy sum each time. The following figures, which represent *halo-halo* sales during the March-to-May period, prove that increased product awareness can lead to a dramatic increase in sales: 8 million pesos

(1993); 15 million pesos (1994); 30 million pesos (1995); 52 million pesos (1996); 75 million pesos (1997); 110 million pesos (1998).

### Changing Negative Perceptions to Positive Impressions

By the end of 1994, we had come to the conclusion that the growth of our company was driven by two market segments: teenagers and adults from the upper- and middle-income brackets. A review of our client profile told us that our patronage by children and families left much to be desired. The problem, we agreed, was that children perceived Chowking as a "for-adults-only" restaurant with little to offer them by way of kid-satisfying food. We also noted that restaurants which projected a child-friendly image attracted whole families, since parents usually left the decision on where to eat to the children.

Given these observations, we set out in early 1995 to develop an advertising program designed to project a new image of Chowking as a food chain for kids. To endorse Chowking, we employed a popular child actor who had a reputation as a food lover. The television commercial showed him enjoying Chowking food. For good measure, light rap music—which children consider "cool"—was used in the advertisement.

In the first quarter of 1995, while this advertising campaign was successfully ushering children, families in tow, into our stores, we turned our attention to yet another market segment—the lower-income group. Market research told us that this group veered away from our stores because they perceived it to be a classy restaurant with prices beyond their budgets. The challenge was to change this negative perception to a positive impression.

So we launched an ad campaign aimed at developing the perception of Chowking as being affordable and within everyone's reach. The television commercial featured a young man with long hair, dressed in jeans and shirt, and playing a guitar. The visual image projected Chowking as a place where one can be casual in dress and manner. The accompanying jingle—which described a mother's worries that her son's allowance was not enough and the son's assurance that it was, because he ate at

Chowking, where meals were affordable—reinforced the message of affordability. The ad campaign translated into a sales increase of 24% in June to August 1995 over the same period of the previous year, with lower-income customers accounting for the increase.

Both instances show that the use of the right advertising material can draw erstwhile non-customers into our stores, overcome their negative perceptions, and convert them into loyal customers. ■

Excerpted from "**Marketing Excellence in Good Times and Bad: How Successful Marketing Practitioners Have Survived Recession-Hit Markets and Prepared Strategy to Thrive in the Economic Downturn**," edited by Jose M. Faustino, Josiah L. Go, and Eduardo L. Roberto. © 1998 by Philippine Marketing Association, tel.: (632) 893 7127, fax: (632) 892 3261, email: pma@philonline.com

The biographical sketch was drawn using the following source:
Roxas-Mendoza, Psyche. "Robert Kuan: Master of the Food Game." *Philippine Graphic:* December 7, 1998.

# Online Resources

- **Featured company**
  Chowking Food Corporation
  http://www.chowking.com

- **Related articles**
  "Market Research"
  From Lycos.com
  Whether your company is large or small, the right amount of financing, equipment, materials, talent, and experience alone is not enough to succeed without a constant flow of the right business information.
  http://www.lycos.com/business/cch/
  guidebook.html?lpv=1&docNumber=Po3_3000

  "The Myth of Advertising's Effectiveness"
  From Nolo.com Inc.
  Aside from assuring purchasers that they made the right choice, comforting CEOs and employees that their work is important, and resulting in unpredictable short-term increases in consumption, most advertising does not perform as advertised.
  http://www.inc.com/articles/details/0,,ART20154,00.html

- **Related Web site**
  Guerrilla Marketing Online
  A weekly online magazine for small business, entrepreneurs, salespeople, and marketers of all kinds, which features marketing tips, success stories, and an interactive reader forum.
  http://www.gmarketing.com/

# Track Consumers' Needs and Fulfill Them Quickly!

*Keki Dadiseth*

*Former Chairman, Hindustan Lever Limited*
*India*

"For companies who want to successfully enter the Indian market, there is no substitute for a deep understanding of the Indian consumer."

**Keki Dadiseth**

Hindustan Lever Limited (HLL), a subsidiary of London-based Unilever, started prying its way into India in 1888. Today, the US$2.6-billion company is India's largest fast-moving consumer goods company, leading the market with merchandise ranging from detergents, personal-hygiene, and beauty products to food and beverages.

HLL is consistently ranked as India's leading company and recognized as the company that others try to emulate. The company has strengthened its position by holding down costs, improving existing products, and introducing new product lines.

Under the leadership of Keki Dadiseth, HLL has doubled profits over the past years with sales growing 20% annually, despite a slowing economy. This comes in the face of growing global competition.

The 54-year-old Dadiseth spent more than 25 years at the company before passing the baton of company chairmanship to M.S. Banga in 2000. Dadiseth attributes HLL's success to its key strength in tracking consumers' needs and fulfilling them quickly. Its in-house market research function—which has existed for more than 50 years now—has received ISO 9002 certification for its operations, an indication of the high standard of specialization that HLL has achieved in obtaining consumer insight. And its distribution network of more than a million outlets across India has enabled the company to gain a strong foothold in rural markets.

In this article, which is adapted from a speech he delivered at the annual general meeting in 1999 and an interview conducted by Dinna Louise C. Dayao, Dadiseth discusses HLL's critical success factors in growing current businesses, expanding into related businesses, and seeding options for future growth.

Hindustan Lever Limited (HLL) makes over 110 brands of products. What ties all these brands together? A deep understanding of the Indian consumers' needs and aspirations. Indian consumers, like most consumers, exercise their choice for products and services that offer superior quality and value for money with much discretion. While this is common knowledge, not all companies newly entering the Indian market have achieved success. These new entrants have found that international renown by itself is no guarantee of success in India, since brands already present have retained markets with remarkable resilience.

There is, therefore, no substitute for a deep understanding of the Indian consumer. The way people live—and their habits and preferences—greatly differs across the country, which has a land mass comparable to that of Western Europe.

Therefore, companies doing business in India need to capture the differences in consumers' needs and aspirations and the barriers and triggers to change. It is equally important to correctly identify market segmentation and competition intensity. Companies must realistically estimate market potential and then develop an appropriate entry strategy with a matching product portfolio.

**Studying What Customers Want**

HLL is able to fulfil its corporate purpose of "meeting the everyday needs of people everywhere" fundamentally because of our deep understanding of the Indian consumer. We acquire consumer insight in three ways. First, we regularly monitor consumer buying behavior through monthly contact with a panel of over 50,000 households spanning the entire market spectrum and all our categories. Secondly, every product—even our communication packages—is rigorously researched among consumers before its launch. Finally, we ensure that our managers get first-hand knowledge of consumers by directly interacting with them.

We convert our indepth knowledge of the Indian market into products or services that offer value to consumers and meet their evolving needs.

In an environment of abundant choice, growth will come from being the best providers of the best value. This means that the company has to develop distinctive knowledge of the entire chain of activities from the acquisition and conversion of materials to the delivery of finished products to customers.

At HLL, we apply state-of-the-art technology to create and deliver value-for-money products to consumers. For example, wheat flour is a staple food in India. It is mostly consumed as homemade bread called *roti.* But the way the flour is traditionally prepared leads to poor quality. Grinding in roller flour mills results in a substantial loss of the wheat's nutritional value.

HLL has invented a grinding technology which retains the nutritional value of whole wheat and ensures that the dough absorbs more water, resulting in softer *rotis.* The resulting product, HLL's branded wheat flour, which is called Kissan Annapurna, is the market leader in India.

We have also successfully developed products that fulfill consumers' new aspirations and still meet their traditional needs. For example, urban consumers continue to oil their hair and yet seek value additions like dandruff control. So we have produced a dandruff-control hair oil, the only such product in its category. Low-income consumers in rural India drink tea not as a social custom but to assuage hunger. So we have introduced a tea-based beverage that contains other appropriate edible ingredients.

## Coping with Distribution Challenges

Developing innovative products is only part of the value equation. Establishing appropriate distribution channels to deliver those products is also essential to any company's success in the Indian market.

Delivering high-quality products, given the state of India's infrastructure, its fragmented retail trade, and extreme weather conditions, is often viewed as a challenge. But we see this as an opportunity to expand and seed new businesses. For example, frozen products are the most difficult to deliver in our weather conditions. In response to these challenging conditions, we have developed a technology based on eutectics for our cold chain. This cold chain is now used for our ice cream business, but can eventually be a channel for other categories as well.

We have invested in a satellite-based communication network which connects our factories, sales branches, depots, key suppliers, and corporate offices in over 200 locations across India. The quick on-line voice and data communication that the network ensures contributes significantly to our working capital management and has significantly brought down inventories, both of finished products and raw materials. The savings are invested in improving products and further extending the distribution infrastructure.

We are also developing direct-selling mechanisms to serve the customized needs of urban India. We have launched a complete range of customized personal care regimens through our network of trained consultants.

In the future, emerging interactive technology tools will help HLL provide even better service. When a consumer uses interactive media, he or she leaves behind a trail of advertising seen, information sought, and transactions conducted. It enables better market segmentation, targeted promotions, and customized products.

By making buying decisions over the television, computer, or telephone, consumers will continuously tell companies about their usage patterns, leading to more focused targeting at lower costs. We have already developed interactive tools such as Web sites, telephone help lines, and touch-screen kiosks for some of our brands. As technology spreads, we will also explore direct-to-consumer transactions for relevant products.

### Managing Growth Horizons

Achieving rapid, sustainable growth requires that we manage three horizons simultaneously: growing current businesses, expanding into related businesses, and seeding options for future growth.

In our current categories, growth will come from increasing consumption and reach. We have many categories—such as toothpaste, shampoo, and skin care—with very low penetration; only four out of ten Indians use toothpaste, about two out of ten shampoo their hair, and only one out of ten uses face cream. Clearly, these categories offer tremendous growth potential.

The scope to increase reach is also large. At least 50% of India's population is not directly covered, since market reach is restricted to urban areas and those villages connected by accessible roads. The challenge for us is to develop appropriate channels to reach the mass market in rural areas. We are therefore putting in place a supply chain to directly cover these areas, parts of which are not even accessible by roads. By the time infrastructure develops, we will have established our brands and will be able to realize their full potential.

To grow our current businesses, we will also need to develop innovative business systems. For most of our consumers, product choices hinge on affordability. Our approach therefore is to find out what the consumer can pay and then tailor the supply chain to offer the product or service within that price. For example, we have introduced systems like replenishment-based supplies and vendor-managed inventory to offer affordable prices to consumers. We are also using I.T. to redesign our business systems in pursuing better quality, better service, and lower cost.

All these steps—increasing consumption, expanding infrastructure to reach new geographies, and developing cost-effective business systems—will maximize the potential of today's core businesses and open new business opportunities. The extensive interface we have built, and are continuously building, with consumers is adding to our understanding of emerging needs. This understanding will help us manage our horizons of growth. ■

The biographical sketch was drawn using the following source:

Sidhva, Shiraz. "Marketing Master." *Far Eastern Economic Review*: December 31, 1998.

The correspondents and editors of *Business Week*. "The Stars of Asia: 50 Asian Leaders at the Forefront of Change." *Business Week*: June 14, 1999.

## Online Resources

* **Featured company**
Hindustan Lever Ltd.
http://www.hll.com

* **Related articles**
"India: The Coming Superpower"
By the editors of *Asiaweek* magazine
From high-tech to pop culture and geopolitics, India is rising in the world.
http://www.cnn.com/ASIANOW/asiaweek/magazine/2000/0811/index.html

  "What If India Had Political Stability?"
By Rob Jenkins
Though some believe that political stability could be India's panacea, Jenkins, author of the book *Democratic Politics and Economic Reform in India*, concludes that stable rule would do little to tap the country's potential.
http://www.worldlink.co.uk/articles/29061999100635/24.htm

# Index